Table of Contents

A Special Thank You

To Howard Kaskel, a member of Quaker Ridge Golf Club, Scarsdale, N.Y., and owner of the Doral Hotel and Country Club in Miami, Florida, without whom this book would not have seen the light of day. For allowing me the use of the Doral facilities over the years, for his financial help and most of all for his encouragement, I am deeply indebted.

In Appreciation

It would have been impossible for me to write this book without the hours of personal instruction and observation I have spent with my father, John McLean, and many of America's great teachers. I extend my gratitude to the following: Ken Venturi, Al Mengert, Jackie Burke, Gardner Dickinson, Jimmy Ballard, Harry Cooper, Gene Sarazen, Jack Grout, Joe Nichols, Mary Lena Faulk, Carl Welty, Ben Doyle, Homer Kelly, Phil Rodgers, John Elliott, Bob Toski, Jimmy Burke, Claude Harmon, Carl Lohren, Jim Flick, Vinny Grillo, John Geertsen, Bob Watson, Craig Shankland, Gary Wiren, Jackson Bradley, Floyd Horgen, Johnny Bulla, Harry Umbinetti, Tom Nieporte, Mike Sanders, Art Bell, plus many others.

To all of them, my most sincere thanks.

Dedication

To my mother and father, John and Agnes
McLean, and my brother, Tom McLean,
who have supported me forever.
Thank you.

The Reason For Drills

It has been said that golf is the hardest sport in the world to play well. Many wonderful athletes who excel with ease in other sports meet their match when they take up golf. The strength, coordination and athletic instincts that serve them well in other games somehow fail them when they try to advance a small ball toward a target 400 yards away.

It is that mystery that makes golf the greatest game ever invented by man. Its difficulties and frustrations are matched in intensity only by the tremendous satisfaction that comes with improving. Accelerating that improvement is the reason for writing this book.

Playing any sport well requires that the pupil understand and execute the physical movements necessary to bring about satisfactory results. The best way to accomplish this is through drills and exercises that ingrain sensations that are correct and reliable when put into practice.

Drills applied to the golf swing are essential—and wonderful—because they communicate feel without verbal explanation. To cure a golfer's slice, for example, the teacher has two choices. He can tell the student, "In order to make the ball curve from right to left, the clubhead must approach the ball from inside the line of play and arrive at impact with the clubface square or slightly closed in relation to the target." That explanation, though correct, is likely to confuse the golfer who needs to *know* how he can transfer the thought into physical action. On the other hand, if the teacher has the student hit balls with his back facing the target (where he can't help but swing along an inside path), the golfer now has a vivid picture of what the teacher is trying to get him to accomplish. He also knows what it *feels* like and can more readily apply it to his normal swing.

Words and physical sensations

are far, far apart. Every human being experiences different sensations for the same physical movement. Very often, what he *feels* he is doing isn't what he's really doing at all. And almost everybody feels motor movements differently. That's why some great players seldom watch their swings on videotape. They know what they feel, and they don't want their mental picture destroyed. They don't want that feel disrupted by analysis.

When a teacher explains something with words alone, the interpretation of those words seldom results in the action the teacher and pupil need to accomplish. Drills are the answer, because they allow an individual to feel the correct movements *in his own way* and he can easily repeat those movements after he commits them to memory.

The beauty of a drill is that it usually is specific to a small part of the swing. Once the student sees and understands the drill, he usually can perform it satisfactorily. With practice, he can perfect the drill and thus change the incorrect movement in his swing—or, more important, ingrain the correct movement.

A few words about how to use this book. The drills described herein cover virtually every facet of the game. Rather than recommend a single, dogmatic "method" that professes to help every golfer, I chose drills used by teachers with widely divergent views on how the game should be played. It is my belief that there is no single "system" that will benefit every golfer. Golfers seem to respond better to some systems of teaching than others and I have tried to choose drills that are simple, practical and of benefit to everyone. Most of them are illustrated to bring you along more quickly and provide a clearer picture of how they should be performed. It is not necessary to read every chapter if some aspects of your game are satisfactory already, although I believe there is always room for improvement and am confident that drills will strengthen every part of your game.

The key to making the drills work is to perform them regularly—daily, if possible. Don't use the drills alone. Incorporate the sensations they teach you into your normal swing from time to time. You'll progress more quickly that way. Once the correct sensations are ingrained, leave the drills, coming back to them only if the old bad habits return.

Enjoy the drills and the improvement that is sure to follow!

Jim McLean's 12-Point Teaching System

This system establishes the principles I use in my teaching. It is presented here only to give the reader an understanding of the basic swing fundamentals and precepts and to give him or her a basis for the proper use of the drills that follow in this book.

1. I stress **Proper Set**, which includes alignment, ball position, grip, posture and a pre-shot routine. I use the railroad track analogy to teach the relationship between target line and body line. Ball position should range from the center of the stance (the spine defining center) for short irons up to the left heel for the driver. I do not teach one ball position for all clubs.

2. I like a **Controlled backswing** with very little independent arm swing—a one-piece, connected takeaway. There must be an immediate response of the body to the swinging action of the club. The wrist-break blends into the backswing motion. Conscious arm swinging in the backswing can destroy a powerful windup and often results in a fast takeaway. I see the backswing in four fundamental stages: Stage 1—The one-piece takeaway, where the relationship at address has not changed when the clubhead has swung three feet away from the ball, except that the weight has shifted onto the right side; Stage 2—Halfway back; Stage 3—Three-fourths back; Stage 4—Top of the backswing, where the arms have swung fully to the top, the shoulders have turned 90 degrees and the hips have turned 45 degrees. Of course, these are checkpoints. The backswing should be one continuous motion. I use eight steps throughout the swing as checkpoints in my teaching.

3. There are **Two Major Separations** in a connected swing. They both occur at the start of the downswing. First the hips separate from the shoulders by turning to the left as the shoulders stay back. Soon after the arms separate from the shoulders and start a free downward swing to the ball. The shoulders and arms must not start together. The shoulders come into play as a result of the action of the arms, club, and hips. The arms and clubhead pull the shoulders through to a complete finish. As a result, the right side (including the right shoulder and right hip) finishes past where the golf ball was prior to impact.

4. Weight Transfer. Your weight should move onto your right side on the backswing. There are two pivot points in a golf swing. Your right leg (the right post) on the backswing and your left leg (the left post) on the forward swing. Your head is not a pivot point. With your longer clubs, this weight transfer becomes more noticeable as the stance widens. Your backswing axis is the inside part of the right leg. As the change of direction begins, *the axis remains* momentarily until the swinging of the arms and club, coupled with the pivoting of your hips, power the weight fully to the left side. As you strike the ball your axis (or pivot point) is the left leg. It is the swinging of the arms and club that contribute most significantly to the

shift of weight forward in the golf swing. A conscious effort to move too quickly left often destroys a powerful hit. In an effective swing, the upper torso cannot lead the downswing by drifting forward as the arms swing down.

5. Swing Plane. In a model swing the clubhead or grip points to the outside rail of the alignment track at all times, except when the shaft points at the target.

6. I teach the **Ball Flight Laws**, which include:

- Squareness of Contact
- Clubhead Speed
- Clubhead Path
- Angle of Attack
- Clubface Angle

It is vital to have an understanding of what causes the ball to react as it does. I especially stress center hits (Squareness of Contact), the one thing that all good players achieve no matter what style or system they use. It also is important to understand that clubface angle at impact influences both *starting direction* and curve, not just the curve alone. Angle of attack also is a critical factor in determining both the starting direction and trajectory of the shot. Also critical is *proper alignment at address.*

7. Balanced Finish. By focusing attention on a pro-style finish, most players immediately improve their balance throughout the swing. Many poor habits disappear with this one simple thought. I have also found this to be an effective playing thought to eliminate unnecessary thinking. Backswing thoughts in particular are difficult to concentrate on during actual play.

8. I do not teach a **High Finish**, but rather a finish with the left elbow folded down. I like to see the classic relaxed finish that promotes speed, connection and balance in the swing.

9. I **Avoid Misleading Terms** common to all golfers. These dangerous phrases, such as *keep your head down, keep a straight left arm, leave your right hand barely on the club, pull the butt of the club at the ball,* etc., usually cause more harm than good. Some of golf's oldest adages must be used sparingly or not at all in some cases.

10. The Left Arm and **Left Wrist** must work properly at impact and through the shot to achieve maximum distance and accuracy. A breakdown of the left wrist on any full shot is destructive to both.

11. I believe in an **Evolution of Teaching**. I teach beginners, intermediates, and advanced players differently, to wit:

Beginners—In practice, they should hit balls mostly off a tee. I stress arm and hand action and minimal head movement. Beginners should see a good swing, preferably on video tape. This will establish a visual picture of the proper motion.

Intermediates—They should learn to consistently draw the ball, concentrating on weight transfer and proper release. In order to move forward (to the advanced stage) the intermediate player must master these concepts.

Advanced—They should spend much time on the course learning management skills and competitive skills. They also should learn to curve the ball at will and control trajectory.

I stress heavy short-game practice at all stages.

12. The whole is greater than the sum of its parts. By this I mean the individual parts of the swing *do not equal the swing as a complete entity.* If some aspect of an individual swing is not technically correct, yet the player is able to repeat that action through natural skills, these instincts probably should not be tampered with. I try to look first for the overall action of the player and the shot quality he can produce. The naturalness each player has can be ruined. A pleasing swing action with rhythm and balance, mixed with natural talent, can have technical mistakes yet produce shot after shot near perfection. The teacher must determine this and take it into consideration before making major swing changes.

This does not mean fundamental mechanics are unimportant. A pleasing swing action that does not produce quality golf shots or does not repeat probably requires technical changes. These changes will take time and much practice to incorporate and perfect.

Practice With a Purpose

For most amateur golfers, who do other things for a living, time is valuable. That's why your practice time should be used efficiently. Too many golfers simply go to the range and beat balls, with no purpose in mind. That not only wastes time but actually can do more harm than good. If, instead, you have a plan for your practice sessions and follow it religiously, you can accomplish a lot more in a lot less time.

There are three kinds of practice—a warmup before a round, a regular practice session on the range and around the practice green, and practice on the course.

The Warmup

Always try to warm up before a round. Golf may be the hardest sport of all to play, yet it is one in which too many players jump onto the first tee with no advance preparation. This almost ensures a poor start and a bad score.

Your warmup session is non-critical practice time. Its sole purpose is to loosen the muscles and find a feel for your swing that day. Concentrate on making on-center contact. Don't worry too much about the direction of your shots except to note how they are curving. That likely will be your shot pattern for the day, so be prepared for it on the course.

Do not try to change your swing during a warmup session. Make only minor adjustments, if any.

The Full Practice Session

After loosening up, work on the drills you have chosen that day to help your specific problem. But always end a session by incorporating the sensations you have developed with the drills into full swings with the various clubs. When you do this, choose a target, visualize your shot trajectory and always work on your pre-shot routine. That routine can be anything you choose that lets you line up the shot, step into the ball and swing in reasonably brisk fashion. But always work on it.

Spend the majority of your time working on the short game. Work on your chipping and pitching drills. Come up with a system for judging distance on those shots. Do your putting drills, then practice very long putts to get a feel for distance and very short putts to develop accuracy with your stroke. Work on your bunker game, doing your drills and playing different length shots to get a feel for distance.

Practice only as long as you can maintain full concentration. If you get tired, your productivity and efficiency will suffer and you'll likely do yourself more harm than good by continuing. If you do feel fatigue while practicing the long game and still want to continue, go to the practice green for awhile and work on your short game until your muscles recover.

Remember, it is better to have several shorter practice sessions each week than one or two long ones.

Most amateurs do their practicing in after-work sessions. Actually, the best time to practice is after a round, as the professionals do. That way you can work on the problem areas that cropped up during the round, identifying your weaknesses and setting up a game plan to overcome them. So try skipping the post-round cocktail and head for the range instead. Both your bar bill and your scores will go down.

On-course Practice

Go out alone in the evening or at other times when the course is not crowded and play two or three balls. Practice playing from different situations. This is a good time to practice fairway bunker shots, shots from the rough or others that you can't practice on the range.

Play your own scramble, hitting three balls and playing the best of them, a game that tells you a lot about your potential. Or play the worst of them, which tells you a lot about what you have to work on.

Or play a two-man competition against yourself, hitting two balls all the way around and keeping score.

Practicing on the course is one of the essential steps in bridging the gap between the practice tee and the actual round.

1

CONDITIONING AND WARMUP

Although most amateurs don't realize it, or pay attention to it, preparing your body to play is as important in golf as in any other sport—perhaps moreso. Strength and flexibility are required to play golf well. As Dr. Gary Wiren, former director of the PGA's educational program and one of our noted teachers, once said, "It's important to get stronger, not so you can swing harder but so you can swing easier."

It's also vital to warm up your muscles properly before each round, although this is a sadly neglected procedure. Too many players rush to the first tee without preparation, then stumble through the first few holes and ruin their scores before their bodies finally get loose enough to swing effectively.

Recognizing the time limitations most amateurs have, along with their unwillingness to engage in serious exercise sessions, I have included in this chapter only a simple warmup procedure and some equally simple exercises for strengthening the parts of the body that contribute most to the golf swing. Following just this rudimentary schedule will help you play better. Obviously, the more you can do to improve your overall strength and muscle tone, including your aerobic capacity, the better you will feel and play.

For example, walking is important, especially on the golf course. Not only will you get a better feel for the game, your legs, heart and lungs will get in better condition. All of this will benefit you in the long run.

If walking is not allowed or is not possible at your course (and, sad to say, it is not at some courses), then make an effort to walk a couple of miles a day at home in the early morning or evening.

In all cases, when doing any exercise, it is important to be aware of your physical condition and limitations. If you have any physical problems, or suspect that you might, be sure to get the approval of your doctor before starting any kind of regimen.

Club-Behind-Back Warm-up Drill

Purpose: Before Jack Nicklaus hits his first golf shot of the day, he does this drill first. It is a superb warmup exercise. It loosens the muscles in your lower back and, with regular use, increases your range of movement. The drill also improves your balance in the full swing.

Procedure: Place a club behind your back and hold it in the crooks of your arms. Now turn gently to the left and right (see illustrations), gradually increasing the amount you turn in both directions. As you turn, feel your weight shifting from left to right and back again. Continue until your back muscles feel relaxed and flexible and you cannot turn farther in either direction.

The Best Way to Warm Up

Purpose: In my opinion, it isn't necessary to be overly concerned with warming up. Don't waste too much concentration trying to be "perfect" by the time you get to the first tee. Rather, you should merely loosen your muscles and hit enough balls to see what your swing tendencies are for the day. The following warmup routine will accomplish those objectives.

Procedure: First, stretch your muscles, loosening your arms, legs, back, shoulders and torso. Use the "club behind the back" drill described earlier . Now hit some easy shots with a 9-iron, concentrating more on feel than on the distance you hit the ball. After maybe 10 shots, move on to a middle iron and hit some more. Finally, hit five or six shots—never more—with the driver. Conserve your energy. Finish with some small pitch shots to develop a sense of feel and rhythm.

Swing On Your Knees To Improve Strength, Flexibility

Purpose: This exercise is very effective in increasing strength and flexibility in your shoulders, waist and hips. It can be done at home or wherever you have room. When done regularly it will increase your range of movement. You'll be able to make a full backswing turn with your body and thus provide support for the swinging back of your hands and arms.

Procedure: Get down on your knees. Extend your arms directly in front of you with your palms facing, about a foot apart. Now turn your shoulders to the right as far as possible, ideally until your left shoulder is directly under your chin. At all times your arms and hands should remain directly in front of your chest.

The muscles along your left side should feel taut as you do this. Now turn in the other direction, so your right shoulder is under your chin. Repeat 10 times. You could include this drill in your normal morning or evening exercise routine.

Turn and Touch the Wall To Improve Your Turn

Purpose: The purpose of this drill is simple. It will teach you to turn your body on the backswing instead of simply swinging your arms and hands alone. The result is a fuller, more complete backswing.

Procedure: Stand about two feet from a wall and perpendicular to it with both hands held directly in front of you at chest level. Your palms should be touching. Note that this forms a triangle with your arms and chest. Now rotate your hips and torso until your hands touch the wall, maintaining the triangle at all times. Return to starting position and repeat several times.

Squeeze a Ball for Increased Hand, Forearm Strength

Purpose: Perhaps the most important muscles involved in the golf swing are those that come in contact with the club—the hands and arms. By increasing strength and suppleness in your hands and forearms, you'll enjoy increased swing speed and more distance, as well as improved control on all shots.

Procedure: A rubber ball is all you need. As you sit at your desk at work or watch television at home, alternate squeezing the ball with your right hand then your left. You should squeeze the ball for five minutes at a time with each hand. Although it is recommended you squeeze the ball for as long as you can, doing it for just five minutes a day will provide fast results.

Strengthen Left Side For Solid Contact

Purpose: Strengthening your entire left side—including your shoulder, arm, hand and latissimus dorsi muscle—is a highly effective way to increase control and improve your chances of making solid contact consistently. The following exercise is good at toning all of these muscles and, when you resume practicing, you'll be able to accelerate the clubhead through the ball with less effort.

Procedure: Stand with your left side against a wall, placing the outside of your left foot against it (See illustration 1). Now, as if holding a club, press the back of your left hand against the wall, making sure your wrist is kept straight (2). Exert pressure against the wall and hold for a count of 10. Repeat three times, gradually accelerating each time.

Swing a Weighted Club to Increase Strength

Purpose: One of the most common myths in golf is that strength isn't important. In fact, the stronger you are, the better you can control the club with less effort. It allows you to use the bigger muscles in the legs, back and torso as well as in the arms and hands. Instead of your body reacting poorly to the movement of the club during the swing, the club will react to the force imparted by your muscles.

The benefits of swinging a weighted club will quickly become apparent. You'll hit the ball farther with less effort and enjoy added control. In addition, you'll increase your endurance and will play well toward the end of the round. Gene Sarazen and Claude Harmon are two great players, among others, who used the weighted club daily.

Procedure: You need an extra-heavy club, preferably one weighing more than 22 ounces. You can either add weight to an old club by using lead tape or a weighted "doughnut," or else purchase one of many weighted clubs currently on the market.

Swing the club back and through slowly but forcefully until the muscles in your hands, arms and torso burn and you are slightly out of breath. Rest for a couple of minutes and resume swinging until you tire again. Swing the weighted club daily. Your endurance should increase quickly.

2

ALIGNMENT

Jim Flick, the Director of Instruction for the Golf Digest schools, the PGA's Teacher of the Year in 1988 and one of the world's outstanding golf instructors, once pointed out that perhaps 95 percent of the shots that are mis-hit are caused by something that occurs before the club is taken away.

Like Jim, all of the great instructors and great players I have talked with and learned from talk about, primarily, setup and alignment. If a player does not set his body properly at address, if he does not aim his clubface properly and align his body parts along the line on which the clubface is aimed, he has very little chance of successfully pulling off the shot.

The drills that follow will give you the basic setup fundamentals and will help you learn correct aim and alignment. If you are having trouble with your shots, this probably should be the area you should look at first. And, since we can't see ourselves, it's always important to enlist the help of your PGA professional to make sure you are doing it the right way.

Use Your Club to Aid Alignment

Purpose: Though primarily for beginners and those with severe alignment problems, this drill can be used by anyone who suspects poor body alignment as the cause of off-line shots. It is perfectly legal and can be used on the course as well as in practice.

Procedure: Assume your normal address position. Without moving your shoulders, hips, legs or feet, take the club and place it horizontally across your

thighs (see illustration). Now observe where the club points. If your legs are aligned parallel to the target line as they should be, the club should be pointing slightly left of the actual target.

Repeat the procedure, laying the club across your feet, knees, hips and shoulders. In each case the club should point just left of your target. By using this drill regularly you will automatically align yourself correctly on the course.

Pointer Drill

Purpose: This is the quickest way and one of the most accurate to tell if you are lined up correctly. It lets you know immediately if your feet, knees, hips and shoulders are aligned toward the target. It is especially useful during casual rounds.

Procedure: Assume your address position, checking your alignment as best you can with the naked eye. Remove your left hand from the club and point to a spot 10 yards left of your target (see illustration). Now see if your feet, knees, hips and shoulders are parallel with your left arm. They should be. If they are lined up to the left, you are "open" and will be prone to a slice or pull. If they are lined up to the right, you are likely to hook or push the shot.

Conduct this spot check often. It is fast and reliable, and will prevent you from having to make some compensation during the swing to start the ball in the direction you wish.

It's Done with Mirrors

Purpose: This off-course alignment and body position check is great for the off-season or during idle hours at home. To do it you need a large mirror, preferably a full-length model. Following this procedure regularly will teach you the correct body position at address and prevent severe alignment problems when you get out on the course.

Procedure: Assume your address from a face-on position, so your shoulders are parallel with the mirror. Now follow this four-step procedure:

1. Look to see if you are relaxed. The muscles in your arms, chest and shoulders should not be bulging or taut. If your muscles are tense, you can't swing freely and fluidly. If they are relaxed, they will be more responsive and will move faster. That means more distance with less effort. Check also that your grip pressure is light.

2. Check your stance width. The insides of your feet should be shoulder-width apart to provide both balance and an ability to turn.

3. Check the position of your hands. They should be slightly ahead of the ball.

Now address the ball so you are aiming directly at the mirror. Check to see that:

1. Your shoulders, hips and feet are parallel to your target line.

2. Your knees are flexed slightly and your weight is toward the balls of your feet, but never on your toes.

3. Your arms are hanging correctly. They should be hanging vertically so there is room, between four and six inches, between the butt end of the club and your body.

Practice Like the Pros

Purpose: To make your practice productive, you'll find it useful to set up a "practice station" prior to hitting balls. By simply laying three clubs on the ground, you can check alignment, ball position and body position. It also makes it much easier to pinpoint swing problems and their solutions.

Procedure: Lay down two clubs, one just outside your ball pointing directly at your target and one along your feet parallel to the first (see illustration).

Now lay a third club just inside your left heel, perpendicular to the others.

As you hit balls, monitor where your ball starts out and the direction in which it curves. By knowing your alignment is correct, you can look elsewhere for your problem.

A footnote: Some amateurs find laying clubs down every time they practice a little bothersome. If this is the case with you, at least lay one club down outside your ball and pointing to the target. You need some indication of where you are lined up.

Select an Intermediate Target

Purpose: Jack Nicklaus popularized this method of lining up golf shots. The premise is simple: you choose a spot directly between your ball and your target and aim for it instead of the target itself. By learning to hit your ball directly over your intermediate target, you improve your chances of landing near the target itself.

Procedure: Before you begin hitting practice shots, walk forward and lay down headcovers along the target line at intervals of 3, 10 and 30 feet. Make sure you are clear of other players before venturing onto the practice range.

Choose one of the headcovers as an intermediate target. As you prepare to hit the shot, visualize hitting the ball directly over the target. Select different headcovers on each shot until you find you are most comfortable with one of the intermediate targets. Monitor your results.

You can use the same method while playing. It is illegal to place an object along your line of play, but you can select a weed, divot or bare spot as an intermediate target. On the tee, use forward tee markers as "goal posts" and try to make a perfect "field goal." By learning to start your ball straight, you'll more often find your next shot playable.

3

THE FULL SWING

The long game undoubtedly is most appealing to most golfers, although, as I have said, it may not be the most important factor for the majority of amateurs. In this chapter there are drills that cover virtually every aspect of the full swing, including the fundamentals of the backswing and downswing and some general drills that will develop a sound swing.

There are drills to help cure the slice, a problem that plagues the majority of amateurs. And there are those that will help conquer a hook that might be raging out of control. There are drills that will help you improve your balance, a commodity so necessary in a good golf swing. Finally, there are drills on the subject so dear to the hearts of most golfers, how to increase distance.

Also, the chapter includes drills on special problems—among others, the toe hit, the heel hit and the dreaded shank, causes and cures.

Among all this information, most players will be able to find—and rectify—the full-swing problems that are bedeviling them. Try them all, then zero in on the ones that seem to help you most in establishing a feel for the correct and effective swing.

BACKSWING DRILLS

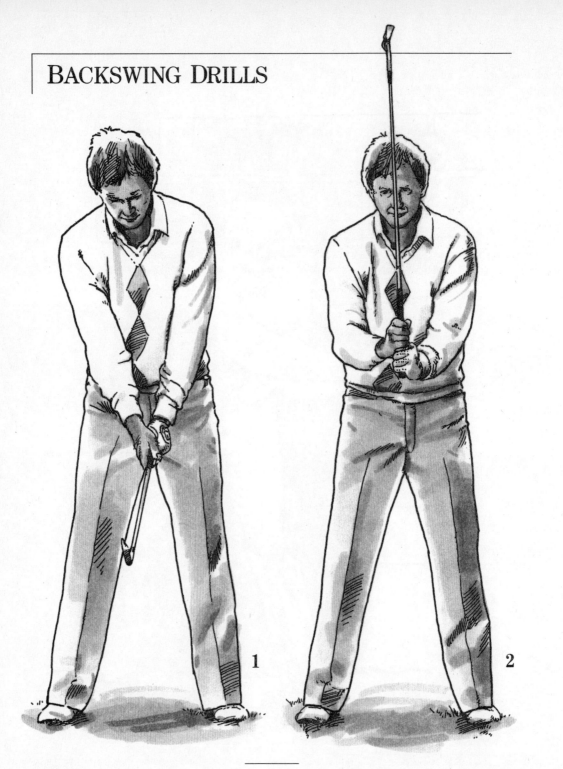

1

2

3

Three Steps to a Perfect Backswing

Purpose: A solid, consistent downswing is the product of being positioned correctly at the top of the backswing. Unfortunately, you can't see yourself at the instant the backswing is completed, so it is difficult to discern whether every feature of it is correct.

The following drill ensures that all features of the top-of-backswing position are correct. It guarantees a fairly straight left arm. It sets the club in the "slot," so it is parallel to the target line. It sets the clubface in the correct "square" position, with the toe of the club pointing almost directly at the ground. It encourages a full turn with plenty of muscle extension.

Do this drill regularly (it can be done at home without fear of breaking furniture), and you'll gain the proper sensation of a solid backswing. You'll then find it easy to transfer the feeling to your actual swing on the course.

Procedure: Assume your normal address position (illustration 1). Now simply cock your wrists upward so the clubhead is pointing skyward (2). Lift your arms just above your forehead. Finally, rotate your shoulders as far as possible, allowing your hips to turn and your left knee to move to the right (3). Hold the position so as to gain a solid impression of the feeling. As illustration 3 shows, you are now in a correct backswing position.

You can actually hit balls from this position by simply turning back a bit farther and then beginning the downswing. Ken Venturi used this drill often.

Practice Against a Wall
for Improved Back and Forward Swings

Purpose: Because the club is out of sight during much of the swing, many players have no sense of where it is positioned in relation to the hands, arms and body. Very often they unknowingly swing the club too much around their body on the backswing and, on the forward swing, heave the club outside the target line and cut across the ball from outside to in. The following drill makes these movements impossible and will improve both your back and through swings.

Procedure: Find a wall and, using an old club, stand with your back to it, your heels about two feet away. Make your normal backswing and try to avoid hitting the wall. If the club strikes the wall on the way back (illustration 1), you are swinging too much around your body. If you strike the wall on the forward swing, it is evidence that you've swung excessively from outside to inside the target line on the downswing.

Ideally, you should cock the club up-

3

4

ward when your backswing is about half
completed (2). This will help you avoid
hitting the wall at the top. On the downswing, try to swing from inside the target
line, making the club swing toward the
target. If your club doesn't hit the wall on
the follow-through (3,4), you'll know
you're making progress.

Doing this drill successfully also demands that you be balanced at all times,
another benefit that will serve you well
when you go back to hitting balls.

No

'Thumbs Up' Drill Creates Model Backswing

Purpose: A correct backswing requires coordinated movement of arms and body. They must work in harmony with each other, or else your timing and swing mechanics are disrupted and you'll be inconsistent. The following drill encourages proper arm and body movement and results in a solid, one-piece takeaway that is simple and easy to repeat.

Procedure: Assume the correct stance and posture. Extend your arms and clasp your hands as shown, left hand below, forming a triangle with your arms. Now swing halfway back and halfway into a follow-through, initiating movement with your shoulders.

At the completion of your half backswing, your thumbs should be pointing skyward (1). On the follow-through, your thumbs also should be pointing upward (2). You should use the same motion in your actual swing to encourage correct arm and hand movement in relation to your body (3).

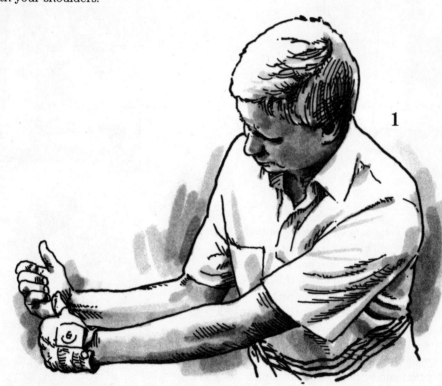

1

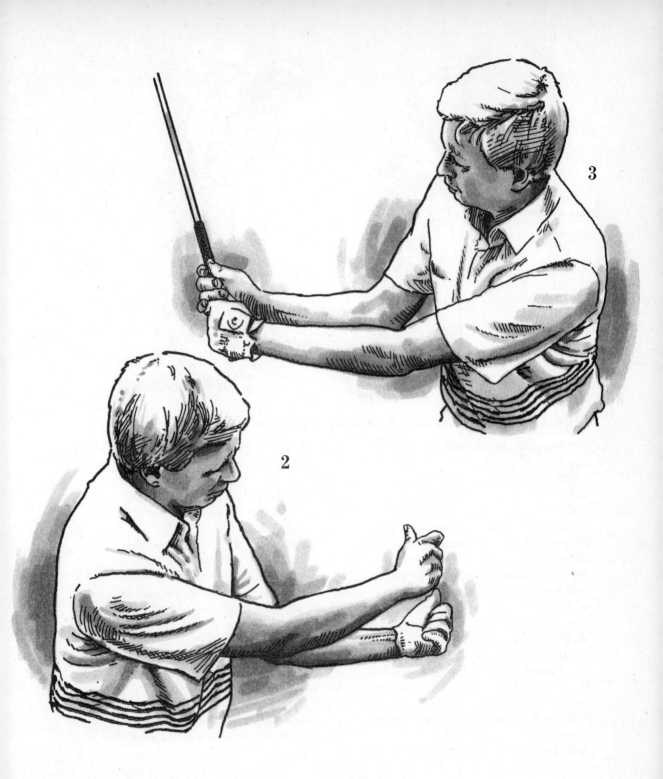

1

2

'Toe-Up' Drill Teaches Square Clubface

Purpose: Perhaps the biggest challenge in golf is to make the clubface return to the ball in a perfectly square position. This is much easier to accomplish if you can keep the clubface in the same position relative to your arms and hands throughout the swing. Poor players almost always manipulate the clubface into a poor position during the swing by twisting their arms and hands, in turn making their impact position inconsistent. The following drill teaches the square position and makes it easy to monitor whether it is correct.

Procedure: Address the ball with the clubface square to the target. Swing the club halfway back so your hands are at hip level and the shaft is almost parallel to the ground (illustration 1). Stop and note the position of the clubhead. The toe of the club should be pointing directly toward the sky. Now swing into a follow-through and stop when your hands are at hip level and the shaft is parallel to the ground (2). Again, the toe should be pointing toward the sky.

When the toe of the club is pointing at the sky at these mid-swing positions, the clubface is square and it will be much easier to return the clubface to square at impact. If the toe is pointing behind you on the backswing, the clubface is excessively open and is likely to be that way at impact. If the toe points directly in front of you on the backswing, it is closed and the clubface will be pointing left, or closed, at impact.

Practice this drill often until you can keep the clubface square at all stages of the swing.

No

Get Behind the Pole Drill

Purpose: This drill will help players who have a tendency to reverse pivot, hanging on their left side on the backswing.

Procedure: You may need a camera or someone to watch you for this drill. Stick a pole in the ground in front of you, as we did in the illustrations above. Have your partner line up the camera so the pole is between your head and your left shoulder. Take a picture at address and at the top of the swing. If you make a proper backswing, getting your weight shifted to the right side, your left shoulder should be well behind the ball at the top.

Triangle Drill Keeps You 'Connected'

Purpose: During the backswing, it is only natural that the arms separate from the body to some extent. But it is easy to overdo this. If the arms drift too far from your body, you lose support from the torso, hips and legs and consequently lose power and control. The following drill encourages your upper arms to stay close to your sides throughout the swing, ensuring the proper blend of arm and body motion. This makes your swing more powerful and consistent and makes it easier to square the clubface through impact.

If your swing feels too "handsy" or "flippy," this drill is for you. It will give you the sensation of swinging primarily with your body, although in fact your arms and hands are contributing their share.

Procedure: Using your driver, take your grip so both hands are gripping the steel portion of the shaft (illustration 1). The grip should be pointed at your stomach. Practice swinging halfway back and halfway through, with the grip pointed at your stomach at all times (2). Note that in order to keep the grip pointed at your stomach, it is necessary to turn more fully back and through, as well as keep your upper arms close to your sides at all times.

No

1

No

2

Club in Chest Drill

Purpose: Starting the backswing smoothly, with all body parts working in sequence, is a common trait among all good players. It prevents any one part of your body—the hands, arms, shoulders, etc.—from becoming too dominant. It establishes rhythm in your backswing and prevents the tendency of swinging too fast.

Procedure: Set up at address with the grip of the club in the center of your chest. Try to begin the backswing "all at once," with the clubhead, hands, arms, shoulders and hips moving away from the ball at the same time. This will prevent an angle from forming and also will prevent rolling your hands and wrists away from the ball. They should remain in the same position throughout the first part of the backswing.

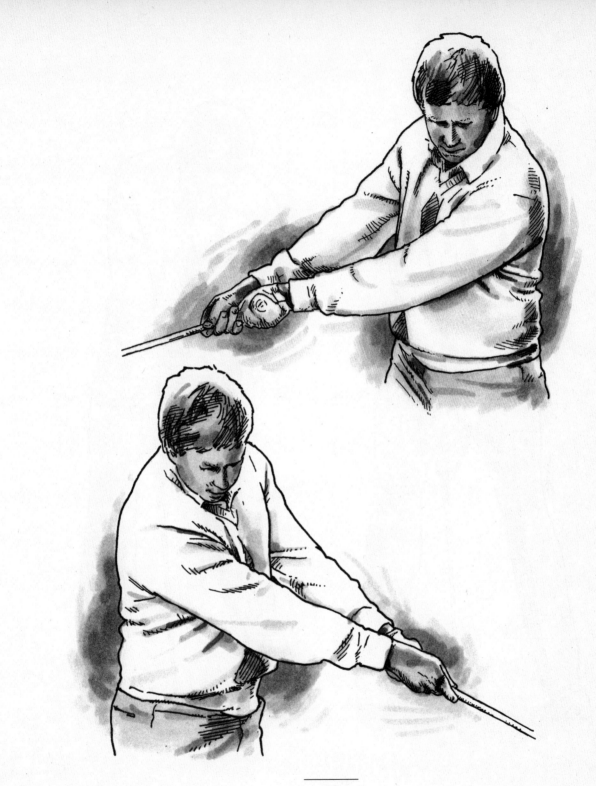

Ignite Your Backswing

Purpose: A common problem among both good and poor players is allowing tension to creep into the hands and arms at address, leading to a choppy, mechanical backswing. Often it becomes difficult to start the club back at all. The following exercise will create a smooth, fluid takeaway that will improve your entire swing.

Procedure: At address, at the count of "One" move your right knee toward the ball a couple of inches, much as Gary Player does. On the count of "Two," start your backswing by moving your right knee and the club back at the same time. (Be careful not to move your right knee back so far that your weight shifts onto the outside of your right foot.) On the count of "Three," start your downswing.

The rhythm of the cadence should not be broken at any point. By keying on the right knee to start the backswing, you set your mind and body in motion and eliminate the tendency to freeze at address. I also teach lifting the right heel off the ground to ignite the swing.

3

Start Club Back Low and Slow

Purpose: This drill has several benefits. It forces you to keep the clubhead low to the ground during the first part of the backswing, encouraging you to turn your shoulders fully. It prevents you from snatching the club away from the ball with your hands, a common tendency among poor players. It makes you begin the backswing slowly, creating a rhythmic backswing that is smooth and flowing.

Procedure: Using an iron, place a ball behind the clubhead at address (illustration 1). As you begin the backswing, roll the ball backward with the clubhead (2). The clubhead should continue to roll the ball until it is well to the right of your back foot (3). You'll find this much easier to do if you try to turn your left shoulder under your chin and keep your left arm relatively straight. Repeat the drill several times.

3

DOWNSWING DRILLS

'Baseball' Drill Improves Weight Transfer

Purpose: A smooth but aggressive weight shift on the downswing is vital in every golf swing. The following drill shows you how to drive off your right foot on the downswing so that at impact, the majority of your weight is on your left foot.

Procedure: Tee a ball and assume your normal address position. Now draw your left foot back so your feet are to-gether. Begin your backswing (illustration 1), but just before it is completed, stride forward with your left foot (2), just as a baseball player does when stepping into a pitch. Try to hit the ball solidly. In order to time your swing properly, you'll find it necessary to swing smoothly, with your weight shifting to your left side slowly but emphatically.

Forefinger Drill

Purpose: Wherever your hands go during the swing, the clubface will follow. If you roll your hands open on the take-away, for instance, the clubface rolls open as well. The following exercise teaches correct hand action that blends smoothly with the action of your arms and body. By learning to make your hands perform correctly on every swing, you're more likely to make the clubface perform the way you want.

Procedure: Take your normal grip and stance, but place your right forefinger down the grip. Swing the club back halfway so your right forefinger is pointed backward along the target line. Now swing through, stopping midway into the follow-through so your right forefinger is pointing down the target line (illustration 1).

Note that in order to point your finger in the directions indicated, you must extend your arms fully on the back and forward swings. You also must "release" correctly through impact in order to point down toward your target on the follow-through.

1

2

Stop 'n Go Drill

Purpose: This drill encourages connection of the arms and body and teaches you to place your arms exactly where you want them. It helps you take the hands out of the swing, makes you get off your right side quickly and helps you feel the lower body leading. Jim Albus, a club pro on Long Island and an excellent player, showed me this drill years ago and I use it a great deal in my teaching.

Procedure: From your address position, take the club back normally (1,2), then stop approximately halfway down (3). In this stopped position, your body

3

4

should look very much like the accompanying illustration. Your weight distribution is back to about 50/50. Your knees have started to move down the line, your left arm is approximately parallel to the ground and straight and your right elbow is close to your side, under the left elbow.

Hold this position for a few seconds then, using your hips and legs, rotate your body quickly to the target. Your arms should stay with your body. Go to a full finish (4). You should feel no active use of the hands in the swing. Your speed is generated by your body rotation.

'Big Mo' Drill Improves Body Action

Purpose: In a good swing, the body responds to the swinging of the hands and arms. This allows the body parts to perform naturally and in the correct sequence. The following swing exercise, which I call "The Big Mo" because it describes the motion involved in swinging the club, will ingrain the feeling of the clubhead merely swinging back and through, with the body reacting to the action of the hands and arms.

Procedure: Using an iron, begin making small swings back and forth, allowing the natural momentum of the hands, arms and club to turn your body on the back and forward swings. Do not, however, try to make your arms swing independently from the body, or vice versa. When you reach the midpoint of your follow-through with your hands at about waist height, allow gravity to pull the club back down and immediately make another backswing. Gradually increase the size of your swings, until you eventually are making full, uninterrupted swings. At all times, concentrate on feeling the clubhead merely swinging back and through.

Drag the Club Through to Improve Angle of Approach

Purpose: Many high-handicappers are aware that swing path is a culprit in poor shots, but few are aware of how important it is to make the clubhead approach the ball at the proper angle. If you swing down too steeply and take deep divots, you'll have difficulty hitting the ball solidly with a square club face. The following drill, devised by Gardner Dickinson, helps you swing so the clubface approaches the ball at a shallower angle, ensuring solid, consistent contact. This is a great drill for good players. It produces the feeling of taking the hands out of the swing going through the ball.

Procedure: Address an imaginary

3

4

ball and take your normal stance, but set the clubhead down outside of your right foot, as I'm demonstrating in illustration 1. Make sure the clubhead is inside the target line and the face is open. Now drag the clubhead forward through the imaginary ball (2), making a conscious effort to close the clubface with both hands. On the follow-through (3), the toe of the clubface should point skyward. Continue through to a full, balanced finish (4), consciously extending your right arm while the left arm folds at the elbow.

This will give you the sensation of a shallower angle of approach through impact and into the finish.

Learn to Release with Body as Well as Hands

Purpose: Although the majority of golfers don't swing their arms and hands freely enough, there are some who use only the hands and arms, forgetting that the large muscles of the back and legs have a role in the swing, too. The following drill demands that you be balanced at all times, and that requires assistance from the bigger, stronger muscles of your body.

Procedure: Find a fairly large, heavy object such as a shag bag or medicine ball and hold on to it firmly as you

1

2

take your address position (Illustration 1,2).

Try to throw it firmly toward a target some 10 to 20 feet in front of you. To do it successfully, you'll find it necessary to coil your body on the "backswing" (3), and drive off your right foot on the "downswing" (4). Note how important it is to be balanced throughout the entire motion.

After doing this several times, hit some balls. You'll be more aware of why it is important to use your body during the swing, not just the hands and arms alone. This is a Jimmy Ballard drill.

4

3

Stop Swaying to Eliminate Mis-hits

Purpose: Many mis-hits, especially fat and thin shots, are due to sliding the body laterally on the forward swing. Good swings for the most part consist of a rotary action with the body, which ensures that you remain "centered" over the ball at all times. A warning here--although this drill tends to freeze the head, in reality you can allow and even need some head motion. The head can move six ways-- side to side, up and down, forward and backward. This drill, which is especially good for beginners, will help you cure excessive head motion in any of these directions.

Procedure: You need a partner for this drill. Without using a club, assume your address position with your partner standing directly in front of you. Have your friend hold your head firmly in place with his outstretched hand. Now make a series of "swings," concentrating on keeping your head firmly in place and pivoting fully. Imagine your spine as an axis around which your shoulders, arms and hands swing. After you have repeated this exercise 20 or 30 times, hit practice shots trying to repeat the same motion.

Play 'Tug-of-War' to Increase Left Side Pull

Purpose: Good players pull the club downward with the left arm from the top of the backswing. Poor players do just the opposite; they usually are too right-side dominant and merely push with the right hand, arm and shoulder. The following drill will create a pulling sensation with the left side, delivering the clubhead into the ball from inside the target line. At the same time, it will improve the action of the right side by demanding that you keep your right arm close to your side on the downswing.

Procedure: You'll need a partner. Have him or her stand to your rear, directly down the target line. Swing the club back until the shaft is horizontal with the ground and have your partner grasp the clubhead (illustration 1). Try to pull the clubhead out of your partner's hand, in such a way as if you were actually trying to hit the ball. Note that your hips and

legs are listing toward your target and that your right arm is automatically drawn in close to your side. Repeat several times.

Now start over, this time having your partner stand so he or she can grasp the clubhead when you reach the top of the backswing. Swing to the top and again have your partner grab the clubhead. When you start down, again note that your hips and legs are moving toward the target. You should feel a tightening of the muscles running from the left armpit down to your side, evidence that you are pulling, rather than pushing, the club into the ball.

Another Drill for a Steady Head

Purpose: This drill forces you to keep your head in place on your own rather than having someone hold it in place for you. It is a good drill to do with your golf instructor, as he or she can monitor the amount you move your head both vertically and horizontally during the swing.

Procedure: Have your partner hold the head end of a club and place the grip end on top of your head as you address the ball. You can actually hit balls with this drill, because the length of the club will keep your partner safely out of range. As you hit balls, try to keep your head as steady as possible (See illustrations). Ask your partner to note how much your head moves from side to side during the swing. If your head moves a few inches, fine—all great players move their head laterally to some degree. Any more head movement than that, however, and you need to concentrate on keeping your head absolutely motionless at all times. This is a drill long advocated by Lighthorse Harry Cooper.

1

2

3

1

2

Put Your Head on a Pillow to Stay Centered

Purpose: Excessive head movement can be disastrous, not so much because your head moves but because your body moves along with it. Excessive lateral sway, along with a vertical move during the swing, is a primary cause of mis-hit shots. This drill, which Paul Runyan advocates and which you can do at home, will help you keep your head and body centered over the ball at all times but allows you to rotate your chin.

Procedure: You may want to use a small pillow and place it against a wall at head height. Stand a comfortable distance from the wall, assume your normal address posture, and place your head against the pillow so as to hold it in place against the wall. Now place your hands together, holding a phantom club. Make a practice swing, rotating your shoulders and torso around your backbone, which acts as an axis. Maintain the angle of your spine, preventing it from dipping downward or raising upward through impact. Repeat several times and do this drill for a few minutes every day.

3

4

1

2

Hold the Shoulders Until Last

Purpose: One of the most pervasive problems among poor players is unwinding the shoulders too soon on the forward swing. By uncoiling them too early, the clubhead is cast out beyond the target line and approaches the ball on an outside-to-in swing path. The result: A slice or pull. The following drill forces you to restrain your shoulders until late in the downswing, resulting in a swing path from the inside.

Procedure: You need an old club—preferably an iron—and a wall. Stand several feet from the wall with your back to it

3

No

and make your normal backswing, freezing your position when you get to the top. Back slowly toward the wall until the clubhead actually touches it (illustration 1). Now simulate a downswing, keeping the clubhead against the wall (2). Note that you can't spin with your shoulders,

or the clubhead will come away from the wall. You should feel that the clubhead is well behind you at all times—which in fact it is. When your hands have started downward about two feet, the clubhead can leave the wall and you can swing through the ball.

1

2

'Bump the Shaft' to Prevent Excessive Spinning

Purpose: This drill, another Ken Venturi favorite, is effective at preventing excessive spinning with the hips and shoulders early in the downswing. It is this spinning motion that results in the classic "over the top" motion with the clubhead straying outside the line of play on the downswing. It will teach you that a correct downswing, with the club approaching the ball from inside the line of play, consists of a blend of lateral and rotational motion.

Procedure: Take your normal stance but slip a lofted iron under the ball

3

4

of your left foot so that it is standing vertical about two inches in front of your left hip (illustration 1). Now make a backswing, concentrating on rotating your hips away from the shaft (2). On the downswing, try to make your left hip slide forward and collide with the shaft at impact (3). If your hips spin excessively, your left hip will not reach the shaft. If you are spinning out, a good swing key is to try and make your hips feel as though they return to the position they were in at address.

1

2

Swing Bow-Legged to Stop Lateral Slide

Purpose: High-handicappers commonly employ too much lateral motion in their forward swings. This is especially harmful on tee shots with the driver. By sliding forward ahead of the ball, the point at which the clubhead reaches the bottom of its arc is moved forward, caus-ing the clubhead to approach the ball on too steep an arc. The result: skied tee shots. This drill prevents excessive lateral movement on the downswing and flattens out the swing arc so the clubhead ap-proaches the ball moving level to slightly upward. Gardner Dickinson often uses

3

4

this drill with his students.

    Procedure: Use your driver and make sure your ball is teed. At address, bow your legs outward as shown in illustration 1. (This is the opposite of what you do in a normal swing, where you want your knees projecting slightly inward.)

Remain flat-footed throughout the backswing (2) and all the way to the finish.

Swing Plane Drill

Purpose: This is another effective way to stop throwing the club outside the target line on the downswing. It also encourages you to swing on the proper plane back and through.

Procedure: Place a ball (if this isn't convenient, a tee will do) partially under a bush so that at address, the shaft of the club barely avoids touching the bush itself (illustration 1). Swing back so the club doesn't come in contact with the bush (2). Swing through the ball so the club doesn't touch the bush (3). If the club contacts the bush (4), it means you've come "over the top," with your shoulders aligned well left of the target at impact. The club also should avoid the bush on the follow-through (5). If you can make the entire swing without touching the bush, it is proof that you've swung down along a correct inside-down the line-inside swing path.

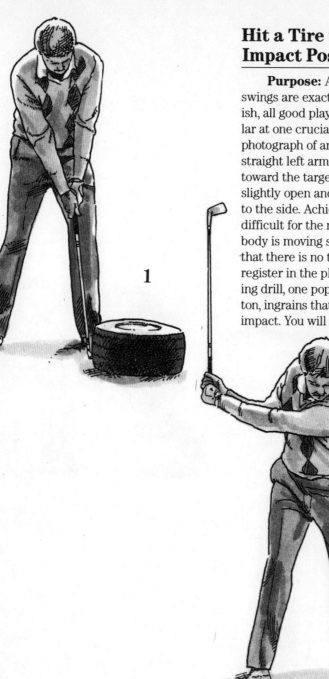

Hit a Tire to Improve Impact Position

Purpose: Although no two golf swings are exactly alike from start to finish, all good players look amazingly similar at one crucial moment: impact. A photograph of any good player reveals a straight left arm with the left wrist bowed toward the target, shoulders that are only slightly open and a right arm that is close to the side. Achieving those qualities is difficult for the novice simply because the body is moving so fast through impact that there is no time for a sense of feel to register in the player's mind. The following drill, one popularized by Henry Cotton, ingrains that correct sense of feel at impact. You will notice that your correct

1

2

impact position is quite different than your setup position.

Procedure: You need an old tire and an old iron club, since this drill is apt to wear out both. Assume your address so the edge of the tire is just inside your left heel (illustration 1). Now make your normal swing (2, 3). Don't swing so hard that you hurt yourself. When the club slams into the tire at impact (4), hold the position for several seconds and monitor the positions described above. If any are incorrect, adjust and note how they feel. Repeat several times until you automatically obtain the correct positions. When you actually hit balls, it will be easy to transfer the correct sensation into the full swing.

No

3

1

Train Left Wrist to be Flat at Impact

Purpose: At the moment of impact, the left wrist should be flat, with no angle between the back of your left hand and forearm. Many amateurs allow the left wrist to buckle through the hitting area, costing them power and control.

Procedure: Find a mound, hill, fence post or tree trunk. Using an iron, gently hit the object, freezing your posi-tion at impact. Do it so your left wrist is flat or bowed outward (illustration 1) and your shoulders are square to the target (2). Don't allow your left wrist to buckle (3), or your shoulders to open (4).

This drill is one of many that also can be done without a club. This can be very productive because it teaches you aware-ness of what your body parts are doing.

No

2

4

Swing a Broom to Improve Release

Purpose: One of the most common problems among poor players is an inability to "release," or square the clubface, at impact. The sensation is difficult to obtain because the club is moving with incredible speed as it approaches the ball. The following drill will train your hands, wrists and arms to instinctively rotate the clubface into a square position at the critical moment. Not only will it make your hands and arms perform correctly and more ef-

ficiently, it will strengthen and improve the performance of the big muscles in your legs, hips, side and back.

Procedure: You need a broom or a wet mop, and plenty of room to swing. At address, hold the broom so it is resting edgewise on the ground. Now make a

1

swing, allowing the broom to fan open on the backswing. On the downswing, the broom will offer plenty of resistance. You should feel that resistance coming from behind you, proof that you are swinging along an inside path. Through impact (illustrations 1, 2), try to rotate the broom with your arms and hands so it returns to the same position it was in at address.

In addition to making normal full swings, actually throw the broom at your target from time to time. This will force you to rotate your hands and forearms as in a real golf swing.

1   2   3

Right Arm Toss Drill

Purpose: The motion of the right arm during the swing is similar to the motion performed when throwing a ball underhand. Emulating that throwing motion improves your rhythm and tempo and heightens your sense of feel. The following is a great drill, one I use often in my teaching, for improving right-side control.

Procedure: Grip a club in your right hand only and address a spot on the turf with or without a ball (illustration 1).

Swing the club back about 3/4 the distance you normally would (2). To start the downswing, take a small step forward with your left foot and then swing through as though you were actually going to throw the club toward your target. Without actually letting go of the club, let it swing through of its own momentum into a full, relaxed follow-through (3,4,5). Repeat several times.

4

5

No

1   2

3

4

Right-Hand Only Drill Teaches Tempo, Release

Purpose: This is a drill similar to the last one that teaches the correct right-hand motion on the back and forward swings. It will help slow your overall swing tempo and help you achieve a full release through impact.

Procedure: Tee a ball and, using a middle iron, address the ball with your right hand only (illustration 1). Make a slow, three-quarter backswing (2) and

swing down smoothly, concentrating mainly on making solid contact. Let the momentum of the swing carry you to a full finish (3,4).

To maintain control of the club, it is imperative that you swing slowly. Through impact, you should feel your right hand rotating the clubface into a square position, just as in a normal swing.

Learn the Hitting Action—Without Using a Club

Purpose: The following drill serves several purposes. It simulates the hitting action through impact, with the clubface arriving at the ball in a perfectly square position. It teaches you to move into the ball aggressively, rather than fall away from it. Finally, it keeps you from placing too much emphasis on keeping your head still during the swing.

Procedure: Find a golf cart and place the palm of your right hand against the seat. Simulate your normal stance. Now make a "backswing," turning your body fully (1). Now slam your right hand into the seat firmly, making sure the palm of your hand is square when it contacts the seat.

2

No

Make Your Legs Initiate the Downswing

Purpose: "Left side control" is an elusive phrase that is difficult to incorporate into your swing. The following drill will do it. In addition to strengthening your left arm, hand and side, it will teach you to use your legs in the swing and prevent casting from the top.

Procedure: Gripping an iron with your left hand only, address a spot on the turf and make as full a backswing as you can, concentrating on swinging slowly (illustration 1). Start the downswing by sliding your legs toward the target (2). You may feel as though the hips are starting the downswing, which is fine, but in any case your lower body should initiate the move down. Swing through to a full finish, allowing your left arm to fold at the beginning of the follow-through (3). Repeat this drill often, perhaps 25 to 30 times daily.

1

2

3

1   2   3

Make an Aggressive Downswing

Purpose: A solid, aggressive downswing demands that you shift your weight firmly from right to left as you start down from the top. The following drill provides an accurate sensation of what a correct weight transfer feels like, and in turn will make it easy to incorporate it into your normal swing.

Procedure: Take your normal grip. Assume a baseball stance, the club cocked back as if you were facing a pitcher, your stance relatively narrow (illustra-tion 1); start forward just as a baseball player does when striding into a pitch (2 and 3); when you arrive at your "impact" position (4), freeze your entire body and then lower the club into an address position (5). Note that your right heel is off the ground and most of your weight is distributed on your left side. After repeating this several times, hit some balls, trying to copy this same position through impact.

4

5

'Quiet Head' Drill

Purpose: Although it is almost impossible to keep your head perfectly still during the swing, it is imperative that you avoid moving your head vertically or laterally more than a couple of inches. If your head moves excessively during the swing, it's a sign that your body has moved as well, and any number of poor shots will result. The following drill, done in two parts with the help of a friend, is unmatched at teaching you to keep your head steady throughout the swing.

Procedure: Have your friend hold the grip end of a club about three inches in front of your head at address. When you make your normal swing , your head should not move forward far enough to touch the club—even after impact.

Next, have your friend hold a club or other similar object at about ear-level at address. When you make your practice swing, have him or her monitor whether your head moves up or down appreciably. Your head should stay in relatively the same position throughout the downswing. You finally can allow it to rise after impact.

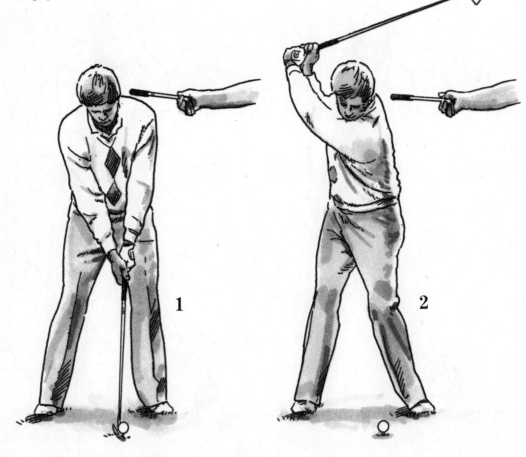

1

2

CURING THE SLICE

1

2

Freeze Your Left Hip and Side to Prevent Slices, Pulls

Purpose: A common cause of slices and pulls is throwing the clubhead outside the line of play on the downswing. This usually results from excessive turning of the torso and shoulders early in the downswing, so that at impact the body is aligned well to the left of the target. The following drill makes it difficult to spin the body too early and forces you to rely on the arms and hands to swing down along an inside path and create clubhead speed. It is a favorite of Al Mengert, the long-time professional at Oakland Hills.

Procedure: At address, turn your left foot to the right so its toe is pointing directly at the ball (1). Now make a practice swing. You'll notice that the position of your left foot "locks" your body on the downswing so it cannot turn excessively to the left (2). Your shoulders and hips will be more square to the target line at impact, ensuring that the arms and hands swing the club down from the inside and contact the ball squarely.

Hit Balls Cross-Handed to Eliminate Slice

Purpose: Many golfers who slice do so because they over-cook the recipe, "The left side controls the swing." They pull down firmly with the left arm alone on the downswing, overlooking the fact that the right arm and hand are necessary to help square the clubface at impact. With no action from the right side, the clubface remains open and they slice. The following drill, which I learned from Bob Lendzion of the Stratton (Vermont) Golf Academy, now head professional at Quechee Club in Vermont, makes too much left side pull impossible and necessitates involvement with the right arm and hand.

Procedure: First hit several warmup shots. Now grip the club cross-handed, with your left hand below the right. Make a minimum of 10 practice swings (see illustration) to familiarize yourself with the sensation of swinging in this manner. You'll notice, in your effort to square the clubface through impact, how important it is to swing aggressively with the right hand as well as the left. After you've completed the practice swings, go back to hitting balls with your normal swing. Your swing will no longer be dominated by the left side and you'll be more successful at squaring the clubface at impact.

Split Grip Teaches Correct Release

Purpose: The primary cause of a slice is an open clubface at impact. The following drill eliminates that problem, as it teaches you to rotate your hands and arms on the downswing so the clubface is square when it meets the ball.

Procedure: Using a 7-iron, take your grip so there are several inches of space between your hands. Now make a series of practice swings with your hands reach-

ing only hip level on the backswing and on the follow-through. Through impact try to feel the right hand crossing over the left. To check that your hands are rotating properly, note the position of the toe of the club at the top of the back-swing. It should be pointing skyward. Now note where the toe is pointing at the completion of the follow-through. If your right hand has crossed over your left correctly, the toe of the club should again be pointing toward the sky.

Drop Right Foot Back to Improve Swing Path

Purpose: Although an open clubface at impact is the primary cause of all slices, an excessive outside-to-in swing path is also frequently to blame. To consistently hit solid shots that draw from right to left, you must learn to swing down along an inside path. The following drill will help you achieve this. As an add-ed benefit, it will teach you to swing smoothly without losing your balance.

Procedure: Using an iron, tee your ball so it is easy to hit solidly. Assume a narrow stance with your feet close together. Now pull your right foot away from the target line about 12 inches (illustration 1). Swing so the clubhead is

traveling along an inside path on the downswing, and make sure your hands rotate the clubface to a square position at impact as in the previous drill (2, 3, 4). Repeat several times.

With your right foot pulled away from the target line, you'll find it easier to make a fuller backswing turn and swing the clubhead into the ball from the inside. After you've ingrained the sensation of swinging from the inside, try hitting some balls with your feet square to the target and spread their normal distance apart.

3

4

Prevent the Dreaded 'Spin Out' Move

Purpose: A common—and deadly—downswing move is prematurely and excessively spinning the body to the left. This almost always causes you to throw the clubhead outside the line of play on the downswing, leading to an outside-to-in swing path and a slice. It also causes your body to lurch well ahead of the ball on the downswing, resulting in a steep angle of approach and skied tee shots with the driver. The following drill, also used extensively by Al Mengert, forces you to restrain the rotary movement of your body so the arms and hands can swing the clubhead into the ball along the proper swing path and at a more level angle.

Procedure: Assume a square stance and address a ball teed in the exact center of your stance. Keeping the rest of your body stationary, lift your left heel off the ground (illustration 1). Now swing and hit the ball without allowing your left heel to return to the ground (2, 3). Repeat several times.

With your left heel off the ground, it is impossible to return all of your weight to your left side on the downswing. That means you can't spin out with your body at the beginning of the downswing, nor can you slide your body laterally. You'll soon be hitting solid, lower-flying shots that start out straight instead of to the left.

1

2

3

Back-to-Target Drill

3

Purpose: An important step to curing your slice is becoming familiar with the swing sensations that produce a draw. The following drill ingrains the physical movements that produce an inside-down the line-inside swing path and a shot that curves from right to left. If you've been slicing due to excessive spinning of the left side on the downswing, this drill is for you. It also helps you rotate the clubface into a square position through impact.

Procedure: Using a 7-iron, assume your normal address position with the ball teed. Now turn your feet and body so they are aligned 45 degrees to the right of your target. Keeping your clubface square to your target at address, hit several balls from this position, swinging along the lines established by your body. Note how the clubhead approaches the ball from well inside the line of play. Note also the tendency for your arms and hands to rotate through the ball. Due to your setup, it is almost impossible to slice the ball. Gradually square your alignment while maintaining the inside swing path and rotational action with your arms and hands.

Think '45-Degree Downswing' to Cure Slice

Purpose: This is not so much a drill as a swing thought. It is useful for anyone who slices due to "coming over the top," or allowing the clubhead to stray outside the target line due to overactive shoulder movement at the beginning of the downswing. It also encourages a flat left wrist at impact, rather than having an angle formed between your left hand and wrist.

Procedure: Imagine that there is a plane set at 45 degrees running from the ball underneath your right shoulder (see illustration). When you swing, never let your hands or arms venture above that plane. You'll find that this thought encourages you to swing into the ball from well inside the line of play, helping you produce a draw. It also urges you to restrain the release of the hands until the last moment, adding power to your shots.

Use Fuzzy Zoeller's Address to Encourage a Draw

Address Position

Purpose: In a hook golf swing, the clubhead should be taken away on a path that is more to the outside than the downswing path. This will encourage you to swing the clubhead into the ball along the correct inside swing path. Fuzzy Zoeller, who won the 1984 U.S. Open, has an ideal way to ensure that his downswing path is from inside the line of play. By trying to emulate his actual swing, you'll learn to swing from the inside and produce a draw.

Procedure: At address, with the ball teed, position the clubhead beyond the ball so you are addressing the ball with the heel of the club (1). On the backswing, try to take the clubhead back slightly to the outside. As you start down, try to loop the club to the inside and continue along the path until after impact (2,3,4). Concentrate on making solid contact.

1

2

3

'Pull Back' After Impact to Learn Correct Release

Purpose: At some point, most players have been told to "finish high" on the follow-through, with both arms extended. This is not good advice for the vast majority of golfers, as it tends to make you try to square the clubface with your body rather than with your hands and arms. In truth, the follow-through should be a mirror-image of your backswing. On the backswing the left arm is kept fairly straight while the right arm folds; on the follow-through the right arm straightens while the left arm folds. Following through in this manner will help you square the clubface easily through impact. The following drill, devised by teaching professional Joe Nichols and used often by Howard Twitty of the PGA Tour, is excellent at teaching this motion.

Procedure: First make some practice swings in this manner: Make your normal swing, but immediately after "impact," pull the club back in front of you as shown in illustration 3. You'll find that in order to do this quickly, it is necessary to fold your left arm quickly after you have swung through the ball.

Now hit some balls, trying to emulate the same motion. You'll find, with practice, that you are squaring the clubface and obtaining clubhead speed by using your hands and arms, not your body.

3

Improve Your Release to Promote a Draw

Purpose: Slices result from an open clubface at impact. This usually occurs due to insufficient rotation of the hands and arms on the downswing. At impact, the clubhead lags behind the hands and arms and the clubface is left open, imparting sidespin on the ball that causes it to curve from left to right. The following drill will improve your hand action and enable you to square the clubface at impact.

Procedure: Using a wedge and teeing the ball so it is easier to hit solidly, hit a series of shots making half swings. Swing slowly and try to feel your hands and arms rotating the club into a square position through impact (see illustration). Once you are able to make the ball curve slightly from right to left, do the same exercise with a 7-iron. Because it is longer, it is somewhat more difficult to square the clubface. After you have mastered the draw with a 7-iron, graduate to a 4-wood. Remember to tee the ball at all times.

Stay 'Connected' to Improve Release

Purpose: Hal Sutton uses this drill as a means to keep the left upper arm close to the sides throughout the swing. If the left arm strays too far from your body, it doesn't rotate properly on the forward swing and the clubface is left open, causing a slice. The drill also encourages you to rotate the clubface into a square position at impact, further helping you start the ball on line.

Procedure: At address, place a headcover or golf glove under the upper portion of your left arm. Hal often practices with a glove or even a credit card there. Jimmy Ballard uses his "connector teaching aid" to make the point. Swing so the headcover remains in place on the back and forward swings. You'll find it necessary to allow your left arm to fold at the elbow on the follow-through. This is fine, as it is evidence that you've used your arms and hands instead of your body to square the clubface.

CURING THE HOOK

For Left Side Control, Let Go With Your Right Hand

Purpose: This drill will increase your awareness of what the left arm and hand do during the swing. It is effective in preventing your right hand from flipping the clubface over into a closed position at impact, and therefore helps prevent a hook. The drill also will help you learn to swing down along the correct inside swing path. Harry Umbinetti, a great teacher from the Pacific Northwest, taught this drill a great deal.

Procedure: Using an iron, make several practice swings, letting go with your right hand at the moment of impact. Swing slowly at first and gradually work up to longer and faster swings. Now actually hit balls, teeing the ball if you find it difficult to make solid contact. Everything about the motion is the same (illustrations 1, 2), except that you let go of the club immediately after you've hit the ball. You'll find that the momentum of your downswing will carry your left arm and the club into a full finish (3). Repeat several times.

1

2

3

Achieve a 'Late Hit' to Prevent Hooking

Purpose: A primary cause of hooking the ball is releasing the club too early. In other words, the golfer rotates the clubface into a closed position before impact, which imparts hook spin on the ball. The following drill, invented by PGA professional Bobby Heins, ensures that you release the club later in the downswing and consequently obtain a square clubface at impact. As an added benefit, the drill forces you to hit down and through the ball, rather than pull up at the last moment.

Procedure: Tee a ball about one inch off the turf. Using a 7-iron, hit the ball so that you make a divot after impact. Repeat several times. In order to take a divot after impact, you must hit down on the shot dramatically, which prevents the clubface from turning over too quickly. It also forces you to shift your weight onto your left side and "stay with the shot" longer than normal.

Aim Left Of a Pole to Learn a Fade

Purpose: In addition to a closed clubface, many hooks result from swinging down along an excessively inside path. This drill forces you to swing from outside-to-in, an all but sure way to start the ball to the left of your target. If your clubface is aiming square at impact, the ball has to fade. This is one of my favorite drills that I use often. It helps players who swing too much inside-out.

Procedure: Find a pole or old shaft and stick it in the ground about 10 feet down the target line (illustration 1). Swing so that your ball passes to the left

1

of the pole after impact. To do this, you must rotate your left hip very early in the downswing so that at impact, your hips are aligned well to the left of the target (2). The clubhead must finish far to the left on the follow-through. This is a drill I devised for George Zahringer, the noted New York amateur, when he was having trouble with hooking the ball.

A key to doing this drill successfully is adjusting your sight line when you look down the line of play. You must look far to the left. When you swing you may feel like Lee Trevino when you do this drill, but that's good—you don't see Super Mex hitting many duck hooks!

2

'No Right Hand' Slows Swing, Prevents Hook

Purpose: If you swing with only one hand effectively controlling the club, you are forced to swing more slowly. That is the purpose of this drill, as it will improve your tempo and gradually increase your chances of making solid contact. A favorite of PGA Tour pro Peter Jacobsen, the drill will give you the sensation that your left hand and arm are controlling the swing.

Procedure: Take your normal stance. Place your right hand directly on top of your left hand (illustration 1). You may leave your right forefinger on the shaft if you desire. Now make a series of full practice swings, concentrating on swinging the club back and through on as wide an arc as you can while maintaining control of the club.

1

2

BALANCE DRILLS

Emulate a Pro to Achieve Good Balance—the Reflex Drill

Purpose: If you examine the follow-through of any number of touring professionals, you'll notice one striking similarity: At the conclusion of the swing, they invariably allow the club to return to a balanced position in front of their body. This accomplishes several things. First, because the spine straightens out, it relieves pressure on the lower back. Second, it makes it immeasurably easier to maintain your balance with most of your weight on your left side. Finally, arriving at this position indicates that you've swung aggressively through the ball.

Procedure: Try to copy this position as you hit balls. With some practice, it will become second nature and you'll find you are swinging with more power and better balance.

Reflections on a Correct Finish

Purpose: This is a drill that gives you an accurate mental picture of how a correct follow-through should look and feel. It ingrains the sensation of following through with the arms and shoulders, not by flipping the club into the air.

Procedure: Study a picture of any great player just after impact. Using a mirror, try to copy the position as closely as you can (illustration 1). Hold the position momentarily and then, using your shoulders only, turn into a complete follow-through (2, 3). Repeat several times.

1

2   3

Swing in Balance—or Else

Purpose: The mark of every good player is an ability to swing while remaining balanced at all times. If you swing too hard, with a sudden shift of weight occurring too quickly, a loss of timing and a variety of mis-hits almost always result. The following drill forces you to keep your balance and maintain a smooth tempo.

Procedure: You need two baskets, boxes, or empty pails. Stand on them as shown in illustration 1 and make a series of swings, increasing your swing speed each time. Find out how hard you can swing while maintaining your balance.

1

2

3

4

1

2

Feet-together Drill Cures Many Ills

Purpose: Few drills are as all-encompassing as the the Feet-Together Drill, which is why it is one of the most popular practice exercises in use today . It promotes good footwork and balance, encourages a free arm swing and prevents lateral swaying on the back and forward swings. It teaches you to swing rhythmically and within your physical capabilities, thereby improving your timing and swing mechanics.

Procedure: With the ball teed, practice hitting balls with your feet touching (illustrations 1, 2, 3). Concentrate on making solid contact rather than hitting the ball a long distance. Once you can hit good shots consistently, try hitting shots with the ball on the turf.

3

Swing Flat-Footed To Develop Good Balance

Purpose: Balance is an essential element of every good swing. If you can maintain it throughout the swing, it is much easier to make the body parts work in proper sequence so you can maximize your power and control. If it's off, you'll have difficulty hitting the ball solidly with consistency and leave yourself open to a wide number of swing errors.

The following drill, a favorite of Ken Venturi and Jack Nicklaus, will improve your balance in several ways. First, it will prevent you from pitching forward during the swing, with too much of your weight distributed out toward your toes. Second, you won't slide your body laterally toward the target on the downswing. Finally, it

1

will encourage you to maintain your spine angle throughout the swing so you won't dip your body downward nor raise it too soon.

In addition to promoting good balance, this drill also will help cure "coming over the top," whereby you unwind your upper body too early on the downswing, throwing the clubhead outside the line of play and causing a pull or slice.

Procedure: Practice hitting balls while keeping both feet firmly on the ground. On the backswing, don't allow your left heel to rise (illustration 1), and on the downswing, allow your right heel to lift just slightly, even after you've gone into your follow-through (2,3).

A Perfect Finish: It's Done with Mirrors

Purpose: Arriving at a full, balanced follow-through is sound proof that you've made a good swing. Building a model finishing position will carry over into your actual swing, ingraining many swing fundamentals with little conscious effort. The following drill will teach you how to arrive at this good finish.

Procedure: You need a mirror or the help of your professional. First, study pictures of several good players in their follow-through, noting how they finish gracefully and in balance (See illustration). Using the mirror, make a number of practice swings and attempt to finish in a similar position. Hold your follow-through for a couple of seconds, noting how it feels and remembering the swing that helped you arrive in such a good position.

Eventually, move onto the practice range and try to make your perfect follow-through while actually hitting balls. Again, hold the finish after each swing so it can eventually become second nature.

DRILLS FOR MORE DISTANCE

Building a Power Swing

Purpose: Many amateurs rely too heavily on the body to generate power during the swing. This drill underscores that the arms and hands really produce clubhead speed on the downswing. Along with increasing your swing speed, this drill also encourages a full, free release through impact. You'll also find it useful as a warmup exercise prior to playing or practicing.

Procedure: Using your driver, stand flat-footed at address and make 20 full swings, nonstop, without allowing either heel to leave the ground. The swings must be made continuously with no pause in between. Try to create the sensation that your body is responding to the swinging of your hands and arms, not vice versa, and feel your swing speed increase.

Make the Club Feel Light

Purpose: To many amateurs, the golf club feels heavy on the back and forward swings, making it difficult to swing it with sufficient speed. This feeling of heaviness is because the club is out of position and out of balance, which also makes it difficult to achieve a proper swing path.

The following test vividly demonstrates how this feeling of heaviness occurs and what you can do to prevent it.

Procedure: Grip the club in your right hand only and hold it in front of you with the shaft vertical. Notice that the club is so light you could support it with one finger (illustration 1).

Slowly tilt the club to the side until it is horizontal (2). Notice that the club gradually becomes heavier until, when it is horizontal, it is difficult to hold in place.

What does this have to do with the swing? Many players allow the club to get into this horizontal position midway through the backswing until, at the top, the shaft is pointing far to the left of the target. Not only does the club feel heavier, it is difficult to swing into the ball along an inside path.

When you swing the club back, you should cock it upward when your hands reach waist height (3). This makes the club feel lighter and allows you to position it correctly at the top (parallel to the line of play). And, because the club is effectively lighter, it allows you to generate maximum club speed on the downswing.

1

2

3

No

Point the Club at the Target

Purpose: To achieve a powerful, repeating downswing, it is critical that the club be positioned correctly at the top. Ideally, it should be parallel to the target line. This makes the club feel balanced, affording maximum control on the downswing. It also makes it easier to swing the clubhead into the ball along the correct inside path.

Procedure: You need a mirror or can enlist the help of a friend. Swing to the top and freeze the position of your hands, arms and club. The shaft should be pointed just left of the target (see illustration), meaning it is parallel to the target line. Learn how it feels and commit the sensation to memory. Eventually you'll be able to emulate this position on the course out of habit.

Improve Left Arm Control for Accuracy, Distance

Purpose: The left arm and hand play a pivotal role in the swing. They are charged with controlling the swing and providing power as well. The following drill will help you develop a correct, repeating motion with the left arm on the back and forward swings and increase your strength. The result: more control and solid ball-club contact.

Procedure: Using a 7-iron, address the ball while holding the club with your left hand only. Make half a backswing, concentrating on allowing the clubface to fan open (1). Hit through the shot, allowing your left arm to fold immediately after impact (2). Repeat several times.

This is a difficult drill to master, so don't get discouraged quickly. At first you'll tend to hit your shots to the right, but after improving your swing path and learning to square the clubface with your left arm and hand, you'll soon be hitting the ball straight—and surprisingly far.

Finish 'Low' For More Power and Control

Purpose: When you follow through with your hands high and your arms extended (far right), chances are you've made a wide but very slow swing arc, costing you clubhead speed and distance. Rather, you should finish with your hands directly atop your left shoulder. Many top touring professionals—especially long hitters such as Dan Pohl and Fred Couples—finish in this manner.

Procedure: Make some practice swings with one swing thought in mind: Get your hands on your left shoulder as soon as possible (1 and 2). Let the club-shaft actually strike you in the back at the completion of the follow-through. To do this effectively, you must allow your left arm to fold immediately after impact. You'll feel as though you are swinging the club much faster with your hands and arms, which is exactly what is happening. Now hit some balls. You should notice increased distance right away and eventually you'll have more control as well.

1

2

No

Rest Club on Shoulder for More Swing Speed

Purpose: At the top of the backswing, the club should feel light and balanced. If the club points to the left or right of your target, it will feel heavier and it will be difficult to swing the clubhead down and through with maximum speed and control. This drill gives you the sensation of the club being in perfect position and will increase your ability of setting it right every time.

Procedure: Without using a ball, make your normal backswing, stopping at the top (illustration 1). Now lower the club onto your right shoulder (2), with the clubhead pointing at your target. Your hands should be about a foot away from your shoulder. Now swing through to a full but low finish and hold the position (3). Lower the club onto your left shoulder and hold it there. The shaft should be pointing right at the target. This drill also helps promote speed by using your hands and arms correctly.

2

Maximize Right Shoulder Turn for More Distance

Purpose: In an effort to maximize the turn, many golfers think of turning the left shoulder under the chin on the backswing. This is fine, but often it breeds tightness in the left side and actually restricts the shoulder turn. A more effective way to achieve a fuller turn is to concentrate on the right shoulder instead.

Procedure: Make some practice swings, concentrating on moving your right shoulder to a point directly behind your head at the top of the backswing. (illustrations 1-3). Note how much longer your backswing feels. Now swing down and through, gradually increasing your swing speed as the clubhead enters the hitting area.

A good way to tell if you are doing the drill properly is to note the position of your left shoulder at the top of the backswing. As you look down, the left shoulder should be to the right of the ball. If it is to the left of the ball, try harder to pull your right shoulder back farther.

1

Full Extension Means More Distance

Purpose: An important key to increasing distance is maximizing the extension of your arms through impact. If you cinch your arms in toward your body, you shorten your swing arc and decrease swing speed. The following drill, devised by two-time National Long Drive Champion Evan (Big Cat) Williams, forces you to extend through the hitting area.

Procedure: Using your driver, tee the ball very high, about three inches off the ground. Assume your address position. Without moving, have someone step in and move the ball 6 to 12 inches forward in your stance (illustration 1). Now make a full backswing, making a full turn away from the ball. When you swing through (2), you'll find it necessary to straighten both arms dramatically in order to reach the ball and strike it solidly (3).

This drill requires practice to do effectively, but it will pay off with a significant increase in distance.

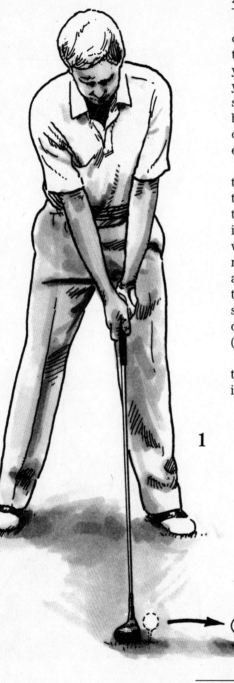

1

GENERAL DRILLS FOR A SOUND SWING

Find Your Best Grip Pressure

Purpose: Discovering the amount of grip pressure you need to swing the club as fast and efficiently as possible while still maintaining control is one of the vital factors in learning to play golf well. This drill will help you do that.

Procedure: Rate your grip pressure on a scale of 1 to 10, 1 being super-light and 10 being super-tight. Start with 1 and grip the club progressively tighter as you work your way up to 10. Identify the change in pressure and give it a number in your mind. Now hit some shots using the same system. You will discover the amount of pressure at which you swing best. Usually it will be in the 4 or 5 range, but it can vary some with each individual. Once you have discovered the correct grip pressure, constantly keep identifying the feel of it so you eventually will use it automatically on the course. Also, try to maintain a constant grip pressure from the start to the end of your swing.

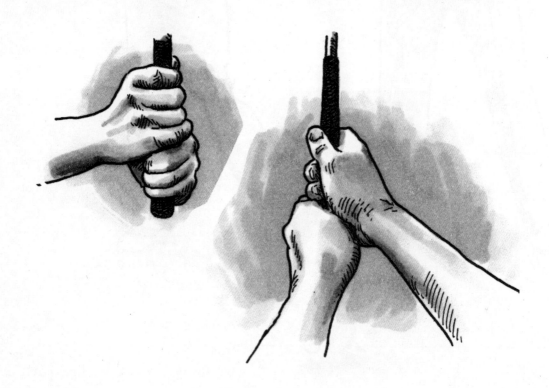

Coil and Uncoil

Purpose: The golf swing consists of a simple coiling and uncoiling of your body. Many golfers employ too much lateral movement in their swings, demanding that their timing be just right to achieve solid contact. This drill will ingrain the sensation of a full pivot back and through. It eliminates excessive lateral swaying during the swing, giving you the feeling that you are swinging around an axis that runs through the center of your body.

Procedure: Stand with your feet shoulder-width apart. Place a club behind your neck and grasp each end with your hands. Turn back and through (see illustrations), keeping your legs braced solidly and maintaining your balance as best you can. Be conscious of the pivoting motion you are making. Follow through with your belt buckle facing the target. Repeat several times.

Make Body Movement Simple

Purpose: It's easy to become so immersed in swing mechanics that you think correct body motion entails a number of intricate, highly detailed movements. That is not the case, and this drill proves it, showing you what the body really does during the swing.

Procedure: Make a practice swing with any club. Feel what your body does and feel what the club does. Now drop the club and, as closely as you can, make the same swing. Now fold your arms at the elbows and make the same swing again. Notice that your body simply rotates in one direction and then shifts and rotates back in the other direction. That's all there is to it. Hit some balls, trying to make your swing and body movement as simple as possible. Be sure to keep your head level. Don't underestimate this drill. It can vividly demonstrate correct body action to all students. Most students are shocked at how little the body does.

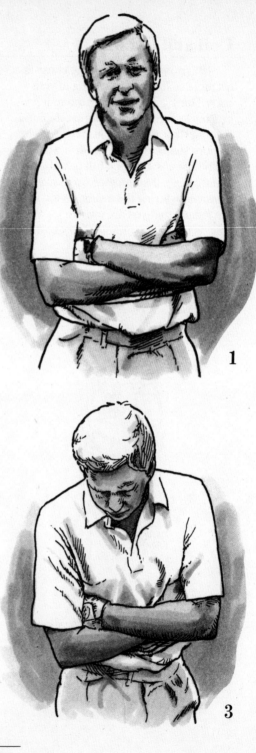

1

3

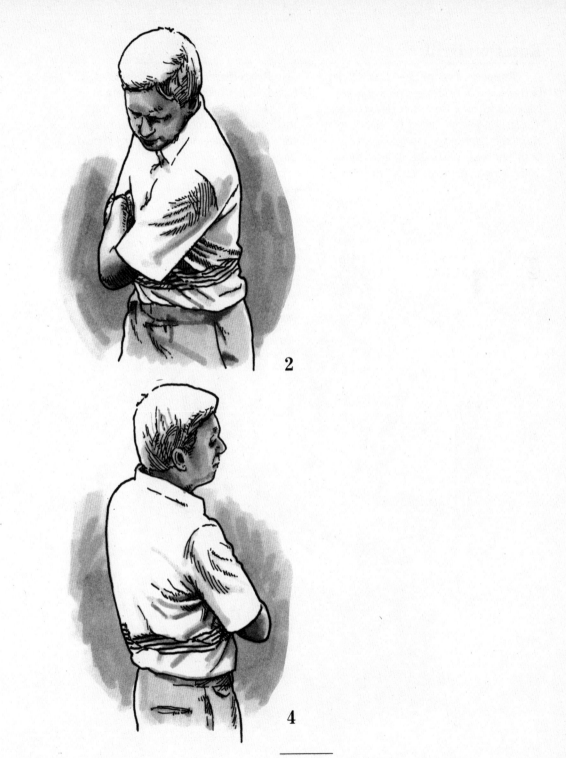

2

4

Rotation Drill

Purpose: I've watched David Leadbetter use this drill when he works with Nick Faldo, Nick Price and David Frost. The drill stops overuse of the hands in short shots, forces you to rotate your body and overcomes the all-arms, head-down action characteristic of the move.

Procedure: Place headcovers or towels under both arms. Keep them in place as you make a waist-high to waist-high swing. Feel your hips pivot through the swing and feel your feet. They should be active.

Learn the Lob Shot to Aid Full Swing

Purpose: The following drill is unmatched at developing feel and coordination. It demands little physical effort but at the same time requires that you use all of your golf muscles. I first saw it done by former LPGA Tour star Betty Jamieson, who claims it is effective for all facets of the swing.

Procedure: Get a large bag of practice balls and go to the range. Using your sand wedge, begin pitching balls over a bush, golf cart or an imaginary object about three yards in front of you. As you hit the balls, make a large but very slow swing, using only about half of your potential power to lob balls over your target. Your grip pressure should be light and you should concentrate on making a smooth, rhythmic swing.

When I asked Betty about the benefits of the drill, she explained that every basic element of the golf swing is included in this swinging motion. The only significant difference between this long, slow pitching swing and the swing for a full driver is the speed with which you swing the club. Practicing this drill often will improve your touch and increase your awareness of how your body parts are performing during the swing.

Make Your Practice Swing Your Real Swing

Purpose: Many golfers are capable of making a beautiful practice swing, only to make an entirely different kind of swing motion at the ball. This is due to anxiety and a lack of trust in your ability to repeat your practice swing when you actually have to perform. The following exercise will make it easier to repeat the swing motion you envision before you hit a shot.

Procedure: On the practice range, assess a shot and envision how you want it to fly. Think about the swing mechanics that will produce the swing shape you need. Make a couple of practice swings until you've generated the type of swing you want. Now step up to the ball, laying aside all of the conscious thoughts you had when you made your practice swing. Instead, consolidate them into one key thought or overall image of your swing. Try to relax and finally, make your swing. How close to your practice swing was your real swing? Did you "let it happen" naturally, or did you "get in your own way" mentally? Repeat this drill daily and soon you'll be making better swings under pressure.

Swing With Eyes Closed to Regain Tempo, Feel

Purpose: Even advanced players sometimes get to swinging too fast, throwing their timing off and causing them to lose their sense of feel. The following drill, made popular by former PGA Tour player Bill Collins, forces you to swing easily and in balance, improving your timing and chances for achieving solid contact.

Procedure: Begin by hitting some easy wedge shots. After you are warmed up, tee a ball and assume your normal address position. Just before you draw the club back, close your eyes and keep them closed throughout the swing. Concentrate on working your hands, arms, shoulders, torso and legs smoothly and in their proper sequence. Your goal is to merely hit the ball solidly. After impact, open your eyes so you can see how close you came to hitting the ball toward your target.

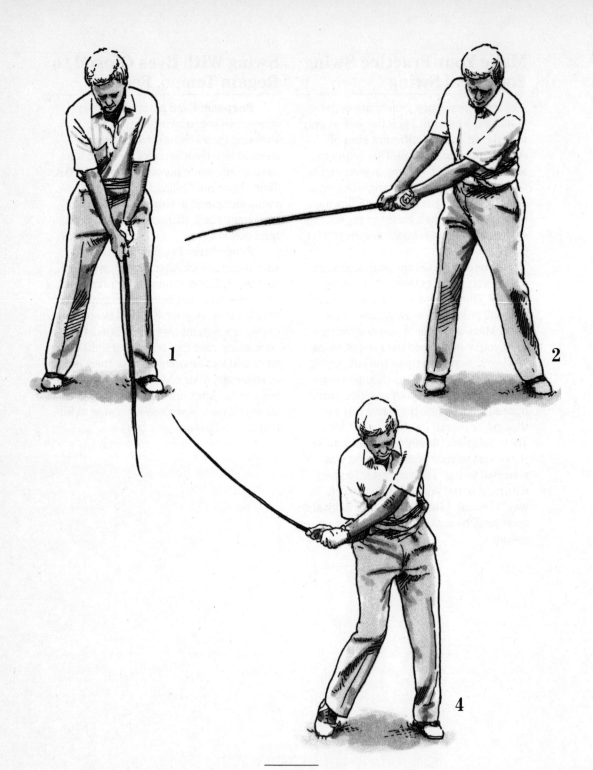

3

5

Swing a Reed to Learn Correct Release

Purpose: An ongoing challenge for all players is timing your release correctly on the downswing. "Release" describes the moment when you uncock your wrists. If you do it too early, you deplete your swing speed too early, causing a loss of power and control. Release too late and your hands will be too far ahead of the clubhead at the moment of impact, causing an open clubface and shots that fly too high or low. The following drill will increase your awareness of the clubhead as it swings down from the top, helping you time your release better.

Procedure: Pull out a long reed of grass or a thin pole or a long, wispy branch off of a tree. Swing the reed back and forth, noting how it lags behind your arms and hands. After doing this 20 or 30 times, pick up a club and swing it back and through slowly, maintaining a light grip pressure. Note how your hands and arms respond to the club's weight and uncock naturally when you swing down. You also will discover the "lag" on the downswing that many great teachers discuss. Eventually hit balls and try to time your release correctly.

SPECIAL PROBLEMS

Toe Hits: Address One Ball, Hit Another

Purpose: Repeatedly hitting shots with the toe of the club is one of the more discouraging problems golfers have. You lose distance, and the feeling at impact is very unsatisfying. Toe hits generally result from an outside-to-in swing path with poor extension of the arms through impact. The following drill addresses both problems.

Procedure: Place two balls on the ground approximately two to three inches apart. Address the ball nearest you (illustration 1). Making only a half-back-swing (2), hit the ball farthest from you (3, 4). Gradually increase the size and speed of your swing.

This drill is effective because it forces you to swing more from the inside in order to strike the outside ball. To further help you prevent hitting toed shots, try standing an inch or two closer to the ball at address, swing the club back on a slightly inside path and finally, keep your eye on the ball at all times.

3

4

Heel Hits: Reverse the Two-Ball Drill

Purpose: The chief cause of hitting heeled shots is allowing the arms to drift too far from the body on the forward swing. This drill encourages you to draw your arms nearer your body on the downswing, promoting solid contact and better support from your body during the swing.

Procedure: Place two balls on the ground approximately 3 inches apart. Assume your address as though you were going to hit the ball farthest from you (illustration 1). Making only a half backswing, hit the ball nearest you (2, 3).

Gradually increase both the size and speed of your swing until you are hitting the ball nearest you solidly.

Some further hints on eliminating heeled shots: Try standing an inch or so farther from the ball, with your weight evenly distributed on both feet. Don't allow your weight to lurch forward on your toes during the downswing, as that effectively places you closer to the ball. Finally, make sure you are not jerking the club away from the ball on an excessively inside swing path.

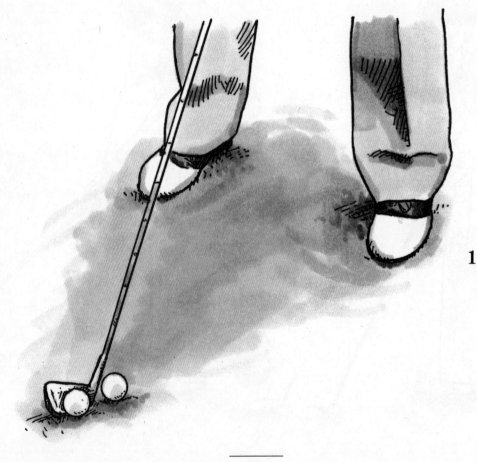

1

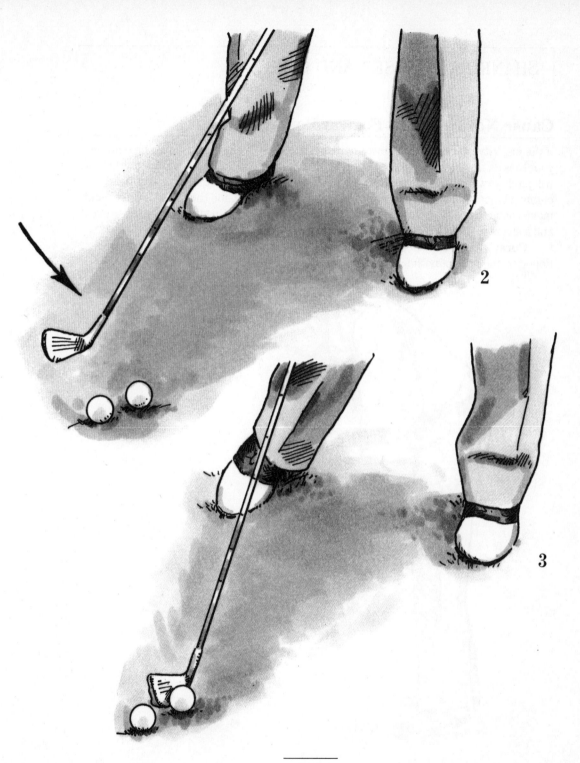

SHANKING—CAUSES AND CURES

Cause No. 1: Weight Forward on Your Toes

If the majority of your weight moves onto your toes on the downswing, your body will pitch forward slightly, causing the clubhead to move forward as well. You make contact with the hosel of the club and a shank results.

Cure: Your weight should be positioned on the balls of both feet at all stages of the swing. It should be neither too much on the heels nor out toward the toes. To learn to do this, place a headcover just outside the ball at address and try to avoid hitting it on the downswing. If you hit the headcover, you have either moved out on your toes or swung down on an outside-to-in swing path.

Cause No. 2: Rolling Club-face Open on Backswing

When you roll the clubface open excessively during the takeaway, the club tends to get "laid off," or on too flat a plane, on the backswing. This gets the club out of balance, and on the forward swing the club loops outside of the target line, causing a shank.

Cure: To prevent the deadly "laid off" position, you first must stop rolling the clubface open on the backswing. This requires that on the backswing you keep your hands in the same position they were in at address. There is no need to roll your hands open. Second, after your hands have reached about waist high on the backswing, simply cock the club straight upward until your backswing is completed. This will make the club feel light and balanced, improving your downswing so you no longer shove the hosel of the club out toward the ball.

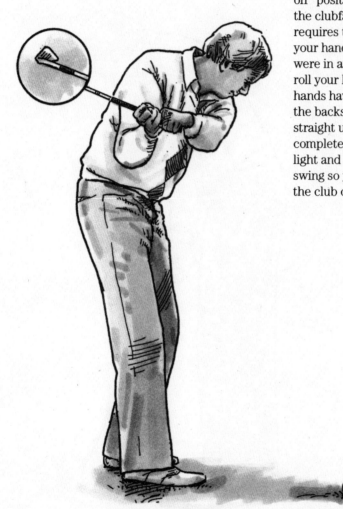

Cause 3: Standing Too Close to Ball

When you stand too close to the ball at address, your arms don't have room to swing freely on the back and forward swings. Consequently the clubhead has little chance of making solid contact either. Due to crowding the ball, you are more likely to make contact with the hosel and hit a shanked shot.

Cure: You need more room to swing. You do this by standing farther from the ball, enough so that your arms hang vertically and the butt end of the club is several inches from your body.

Cause 4: Sliding Body Ahead of Ball on Downswing

When you employ too much lateral motion on the forward swing, your body moves ahead of the ball and leaves the hands, arms and clubhead trailing behind (See illustration). The clubhead approaches the ball too much from the inside and the clubface is open. These factors lead you to strike the ball with the hosel.

Cure: Try to achieve a more relaxed swinging action, with minimal grip pressure and no tension in your arms at address. Try to make a long, slow backswing, keeping your head steady at all times. This will make it easier to return the clubface to the same position it was in at address and you'll make on-center contact more often.

For Reverse Pivot: Hit Balls on an Upslope

Purpose: The classic reverse pivot consists of putting too much weight on your left, or forward foot on the backswing, and then falling back on your right foot during the downswing. This drill is effective because it helps you transfer your weight onto your right foot on the backswing.

Procedure: Find an upslope. Hit balls, maintaining a smooth rhythm at all

times. Note that on the backswing, gravity
tends to make you shift the majority of
your weight onto your right foot. This is
what the weight shift should feel like
when you are playing off level lies.

'Walk Through the Shot' to Cure Reverse Pivot

Purpose: There's no better cure for a reverse pivot than doing this drill. It makes it impossible to finish with your weight on your right side. By improving your weight transfer, you'll make a more assertive downswing and obtain greater power and accuracy.

Procedure: Tee a ball to increase your chances of making solid contact. Using an iron, assume your normal address position and make a conventional backswing. Just after impact on the downswing, step down the fairway with your right foot (2, 3).

A number of fine professionals, including Chi Chi Rodriguez and Gary Player, make this move as part of their normal swing. It not only prevents a reverse pivot but helps you obtain a full release with your body as well as with your arms and hands.

1

2

3

Topped Shots: Learn Correct Weight Transfer

Purpose: When you hang back on your right side on the forward swing, the clubhead tends to reach the lowest point of its arc well before it reaches the ball. It is actually ascending, or moving upward, at impact, and a topped shot results. The following drill will help you shift your weight onto the left leg and foot on the downswing and help you make the descending blow you need with an iron.

Procedure: Place a headcover, golf tee or other object on your target line about one foot behind your ball. Now, using a short iron, hit the ball while trying to avoid hitting the headcover. If you hang back on your right side, you'll hit the headcover due to the clubhead bottoming out too soon. But if you shift your weight onto your left foot, the clubhead will avoid the headcover and strike the ball you are aiming for. You'll make a descending blow and take a divot after impact.

Can You Move Away From the Wall?

Purpose: Here is a fast, simple check to see that you are shifting your weight onto your right side on the backswing.

Procedure: Address the ball while standing with your left foot placed against a wall (illustration 1). Now make a backswing, taking care not to let the clubhead strike the wall at the top. If you are shifting your weight correctly, your body will have moved one foot away from the wall (2). If your left side remains close to the wall, you need to concentrate on shifting your weight more emphatically onto your right side.

4

THE SHORT GAME

I f you are serious about improving your golf game and lowering your scores, follow my 90/10 formula—that is, spend 10 percent of your practice time on the long game and 90 percent on the short game, including pitching, chipping, bunker play and putting.

Chipping and pitching are by far the most underrated phases of the game. Practicing this part of the game and building a technique that is fundamentally sound not only will save you a lot of strokes when you miss a green (and we all miss a lot of them in the course of a round) but also will improve your full swing. That's because the chipping and pitching swings are miniature versions of the full swing. Chipping incorporates correct swing path and correct clubface angle, position of the left wrist at impact and the relationship between the clubhead, hands and body through the hitting area, the same factors you must deal with in the long game.

So training yourself to repeat a simple chipping action with correct fundamentals is the best way to correct major faults in your full swing. The mistakes that show up in chipping will be magnified in your full swing. Conversely, the proper technique ingrained into your chipping stroke will show up in the big swing (without much effort on your part).

Anyone can learn proper chipping fundamentals with discipline and dedication. Admittedly, this will take time, but it is the shortest path to stroke-saving around the greens and full-swing improvement as well.

Putting is equally important, if not moreso. Studies have determined that putting comprises between 40 and 45 percent of all strokes taken during a round. Therefore, if you improve your putting you will lower your scores—certainly more than you could with the same percentage of improvement in other phases of the game.

The problem I see is that not many people will take the time to practice the short game. Even if they realize the importance of it, golfers are not usually willing to put in enough time on it. They see short-game practice as boring and tedious.

The solution: You must make short-game practice fun. I have included a large number of pitching, chipping and putting drills in this chapter, as well as a couple of drills that will help you escape the dreaded bunkers. Hopefully some of these will appeal to you. If you can make a game out of short-game practice, the time will pass quickly and your golf scores will drop significantly.

Try it and see if that doesn't happen.

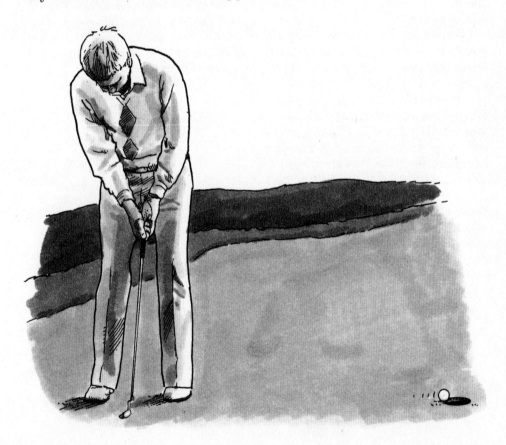

PITCHING AND CHIPPING

Develop a Formula for Different Clubs

Purpose: Many players resort to using the same club on all chip shots, particularly when they are under pressure. This is not a very effective method, because it is difficult to regulate how far the ball travels in the air and how far it rolls after landing. For consistent, predictable chip shots, I recommend you use different clubs depending on your lie, the slope and speed of the green and the feel you have on a given day.

With practice, you can accurately judge how far the ball carries and rolls with different clubs, widening your repertoire of shots around the greens.

Procedure: Take a pitching wedge, 8-iron, 7-iron and 6-iron to the practice green. Find a patch of turf that is level with the green and hit one chip with each club. Repeat several times, giving each club equal attention. Make sure you use the same chipping motion with each club, noting how far the ball carries and rolls with the different irons.

You'll find you can develop your own "chipping calculus" that will help you determine how the ball behaves on each one. A typical formula:

Pitching Wedge—1/2 air time, 1/2 ground time.

8-iron—1/3 air time, 2/3 ground time.

7-iron—1/4 air time, 3/4 ground time.

6-iron—1/5 air time, 4/5 ground time.

Your own formula will vary, of course. Your choice of clubs on specific chips will vary due to factors such as terrain, but you'll soon be able to choose the club that gives you the best chance of chipping the ball close to the hole.

Circle Drill Teaches How Far Shots Fly, Roll

Purpose: This drill is effective for both chips and pitches. It provides you with a vivid picture of how far the ball flies and rolls with different clubs. It emphasizes that it isn't necessary to land the ball on a precise spot on the green to obtain a good result. Rather, if you can land the ball within an imaginary six-foot circle, you are assured of a reasonably accurate chip or pitch.

Procedure: Designate a target on the green and, through trial and error, find the spot on the green where the ball must land in order to roll close to the hole. Now lay some string in a six-foot circle around the spot. Practice landing your shots somewhere within the circle and letting the ball roll near the hole. When you get on the course, picture in your mind's eye the imaginary circle and try to land your ball within it.

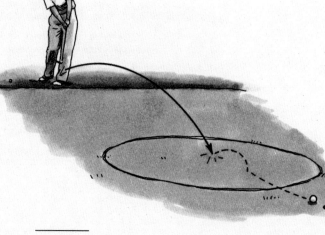

'Big Breaker' Drill Helps On Sloping Greens

Purpose: Chipping across a severely sloped green is one of the most difficult shots in the game. The best way to do it is to imagine the path the ball will take after landing on the green, and then hit the chip at the point where the ball began to break. Determining this point takes imagination and feel, but the following drill will make it easier. If you do it often, you'll be able to accurately judge the break and hit the chip with the speed required to make it die near the hole.

Procedure: Select a hole positioned on a sideslope. Scatter several balls near the green and chip toward the hole, mentally marking the spot where the ball began to break. Now hit several chips while aiming at the spot where the ball started to break. Try to hit the shot with the speed necessary to make the ball break as you pictured it.

Punch-Shot Drill to Make Hands Lead

Purpose: On every shot in golf, the hands arrive at the ball before the clubhead. Letting the clubhead pass the hands on the downswing leads to mis-hits and inconsistency. This drill, executed with the help of a friend, helps you lead with your hands not only on chips and pitches, but on full-swing shots as well. I learned this terrific drill from Claude Harmon.

Procedure: Using a 7-iron, set yourself up with a very short chip shot. Address the ball normally, making sure that your hands are slightly ahead of the ball. Make a small backswing. Just before you start down, have your partner place the grip end of a club just in front of the ball. Hit the chip, letting your partner's club stop your clubhead just after impact.

The moment your clubhead is stopped by the grip end of your partner's club, freeze your position. Note that your hands are ahead of the ball. Memorize the sensation. Repeat several times and then practice without help from your partner. Soon you'll be leading with your hands on every shot.

1

2

3

1

2

Freeze Your Wrists for Solid Contact

Purpose: On shots requiring a short swing, you want to eliminate as much excess movement in the swing as possible. The following drill, a favorite of Ken Venturi, makes your pitching swing a simple action that results in greater consistency.

Procedure: Scatter some balls a few feet near the practice green. Address one with your feet and knees aligned to the left of your target, with most of your weight positioned on your left foot (illustration 1).

Make a short backswing, imagining your wrists are in a cast to eliminate any flippy movement with your hands and wrists (2). Make a descending blow with the clubhead and pinch the ball from the turf (3). Don't try to scoop the ball in an

3　　　　　4　　　　　5

effort to get it airborne. Through impact,
don't let your right hand cross over your
left. Maintain the flex in your knees at all
times (4,5).

By eliminating unwanted hinging of the
wrists, the clubhead approaches the ball
at a relatively flat angle, decreasing your
margin for error.

Trough Drill Helps Keep Chips on Line

Purpose: This drill is great at improving your chipping stroke so you can make solid contact and hit your chips on the intended line every time. By hitting your chips solidly, you'll get maximum distance with your chipping stroke, eliminating undue effort on longer chip shots.

Procedure: Take two clubs and form a narrow trough (illustration 1). Using a 7-iron, practice making a perfect chipping stroke, with the clubhead traveling only slightly inside the line of play on the backswing and finishing low to the ground and in the middle of the trough on the follow-through.

Now hit some chips shots to a hole

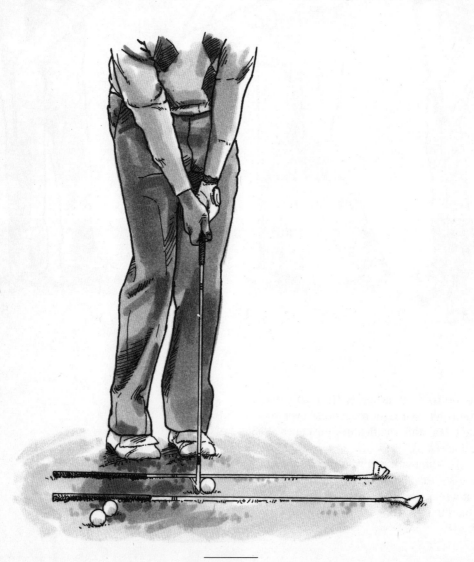

about 10 feet from the edge of the green, making a very small backswing and accelerating the clubhead through the ball. Make sure the clubhead finishes low to the ground at the finish of the stroke (2), with the toe of the clubhead closing slightly. The clubhead should be extended straight down the line of play.

Gradually increase the distance of the target and the size of your swing. This drill successfully teaches: 1) clubface control; 2) correct swing path; and 3) proper angle of attack.

BUNKER DRILLS

The Venturi Tee Drill

Purpose: This is a drill used by former U.S. Open Champion Ken Venturi, a superb bunker player and teacher of sand play. It teaches you to make a shallow cut through the sand with your club rather than swinging too steeply into the sand, gouging out a pile of it and often leaving your ball in the bunker. Making a shallower cut through the sand will get the ball out more consistently and give you better control of the shot from all types of sand.

Procedure: Place your ball on a tee in the sand, then push the tee into the sand so that the head of the tee is barely above the surface. Position the ball off your left heel and use a slightly wider-than-normal stance. Then try to clip the head off the tee. To do this you will find you have to hit behind the ball with a shallow angle of approach, "slipping" the club under the ball. The swing requires very little wrist action—instead, think of sweeping the club back and through as you clip the head off that tee.

In actual play, imagine the tee sitting under the ball and try to make the same swing.

By varying how much you open the face of the club you can control the distance of the shot. The length of your backswing and followthrough also is a major determinant of distance.

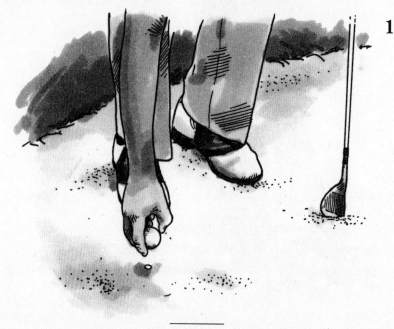

1

Greenside Bunker Drill

Purpose: This drill works miracles. It gives you a sense of splashing the ball out of the sand. It teaches that you must not hit the ball but instead must cut a large and shallow swath of sand out from under the ball....and that you must complete your swing. It also tells you don't have to be perfect in the sand, that you have a margin for error greater than most other shots in golf.

Once you can make this shot five times in a row in practice, you will successfully hit your first bunker shot on the course. . . . I'll virtually guarantee it.

Procedure: With the toe of your sand wedge, draw two lines in the sand

about 10 inches apart and perpendicular to your target line. Take practice swings and cut out swaths of sand between the two lines, the club entering the sand in front of the back line and leaving the sand behind the front line. Finish your swing.

When you can make five swings in a row between the lines, place a ball two or three inches behind the front line. Then make your swing at the ball with the exact thought process you had when the ball wasn't there.

Get five straight balls out of the sand in this manner and head for the course. But keep practicing regularly.

3

4

Rake Drill

Purpose: This drill is to help you develop a feel for the upright swing that is necessary to hit proper bunker shots. It forces you to cock the club up early on the backswing and create more of a V-shaped swing. Claude Harmon, regarded as probably the greatest teacher of the bunker game in America, used this drill to get quick results with his students.

Procedure: You need someone to hold a rake approximately two feet behind your ball on about a 45-degree angle (see illustration). The idea is to swing the club up the rake handle. This will feel like it is a very abrupt pickup at first. In fact, it is the correct method that allows you to get the club under the ball and to use the flange of the sand wedge correctly.

Take several backswings and downswings without hitting the ball to get the feel of your swing shape. Then hit some balls while your partner holds the rake.

Remember to make a full shoulder turn both ways and to finish your swing. You should be hitting high, soft bunker shots in short order.

Erase the Footprint

Purpose: This is a drill that I got from Al Mengert, that again will ingrain the sensation of making the proper shallow cut through the sand, giving you more spin and better control of the ball as you splash it out of the bunker.

Procedure: Lightly make some footprints in the sand. Then make practice swings, simply trying to erase those footprints. Do not slam your club down into the sand. Just try to lightly brush through the length of the footprint with the flange or bottom of your club.

Now place a ball in the center of the footprint and try to make the same swing, concentrating simply on erasing the footprint. You will be amazed and gratified at the consistency with which the ball comes out.

Fairway Bunker Fundamentals

Purpose: This is more of a mental than a physical drill, but working on it will help you successfully escape fairway bunkers during an actual round.

Procedure: First and foremost, pick a club that will comfortably get the ball over the lip of the bunker. If the club you choose will get you to the green, fine, but you first have to get out of the bunker.

Always pick one club longer than necessary (assuming that it will get you over the lip). You always want to swing well within yourself for better control, just picking the ball off the sand, so that the shot will not travel as far as normal.

Position the ball in the middle or slightly forward in your stance. Plant your feet firmly in the sand and eliminate unnecessary lower-body action. The swing is made primarily with the arms and upper body. Try to pick the ball clean, playing the shot as if you are going to half top it. Pretend you are setting up to hit a driver and pick the ball off in a "sweeping motion." The worst mistake you can make is to hit behind the ball.

PUTTING

'Watch the Dot' On Short Putts

Purpose: Johnny Miller won the 1976 British Open with this putting method. While you may not actually want to putt in this manner, it does make an excellent practice exercise because it prevents you from focusing too intently on the putterface during the stroke. If you feel you have the "yips," tend to jab at the ball or simply putt the short ones poorly, this exercise will help.

Procedure: Paint a white dot on the bottom of your putter grip so you can see it clearly when you address the ball. Now putt a series of 3-foot putts, concentrating on the white dot. Try to make it move in a straight-back, straight-through manner.

Because you can't see the ball during the stroke, you remove the anxiety that comes from looking at the ball or the putterface. You'll learn to make a smooth, even stroke and use your sense of feel to keep the putterface square through impact.

Putt With Eyes Closed for Smoother Stroke

Purpose: Here is another effective way to make your putting stroke soft and smooth. This drill will shift your attention away from the mechanics of the stroke and force you to concentrate on feel. The urge to lift your head too soon to see where the ball is going will vanish. The result: less anxiety on putts of all distances.

Procedure: Hit a series of 10-foot putts with your eyes closed. Make sure you are settled in correctly at address. Concentrate on hitting the putt solidly with an accelerating motion on the forward stroke and with an ultra-smooth stroke.

Widen Stance When Putting In the Wind

Purpose: Wind can wreak as much havoc with your putting stroke as it can on full-swing shots. Balance is extremely important in putting and a strong breeze can make it very difficult to remain perfectly still over the ball. The following method is used by many players to keep their body steady when it's windy.

Procedure: Widen your stance (see illustration). This will give you more balance and support from your lower body, ensuring that your arms, shoulders and head remain still during the stroke. Widening your stance also positions your body lower to the ground, lessening the effect of the wind.

The Advantages of Putting Cross-Handed

Purpose: Many good players, including Bruce Lietzke and Bernhard Langer, suffered from poor putting only to be reborn by trying the cross-handed method. It accomplishes several things that a conventional putting grip does not. First, it prevents your left hand and wrist from hinging or breaking down through impact. Second, it helps keep your shoulders level at address and at impact. This serves to keep the putter low to the ground on the follow-through, which is much better than lifting it off the ground abruptly after contact. Next, it gives you the feeling that the left hand and arm are controlling the stroke. Putting conventionally, many players have the feeling that the right hand "takes over," resulting in poor direction and distance control.

Procedure: Simply grasp the putter as I'm doing in the illustration. Concentrate on making a slow, smooth stroke. Give the method plenty of time.

Look At the Hole to Make Smoother Stroke

Purpose: Another way to eliminate the tendency to be too "ball conscious" during the stroke is to look at the hole while you putt. By shifting your attention to the hole rather than the ball or the putter, you'll make a smoother, less-mechanical stroke.

Procedure: Assume your normal putting stance and address position. Make sure the putter is aligned squarely at the hole before you initiate the stroke. Now look at the hole and don't allow your eyes to drift away from it. Imagine how hard you must strike the ball to make it roll the correct distance. Now stroke the putt (see illustration), monitoring where the ball goes and adjusting your setup or stroke as necessary to improve your accuracy.

Use a Mirror to Check Fundamentals

Purpose: It is discouragingly easy to get away from the fundamentals in all areas of the game. With putting, the areas that most often go astray are the positions of the hands, the alignment of the putterface and the position of your eyes in relation to the ball. The following exercise allows you to check all three in just a few minutes.

Procedure: Get a small mirror (it should be at least 4" by 12") and lay it lengthwise on the green so it is parallel to your target line. Draw a straight line at each end of the mirror, perpendicular to the target line. Now lay a ball on the mirror and address it normally.

Looking down, first check to see that your eyes are directly over the ball. Now check the putterface to see that it is aligned squarely to the target.

Finally, examine the position of your hands. They should be even or slightly ahead of the ball, never behind. Start over and repeat the process several times until your fundamentals are correct. Remove the mirror and emulate the correct positions.

Five-In-A-Line Drill
Promotes Consistency

Purpose: The following drill is a great way to sharpen your concentration and make yourself more immune to pressure.

Procedure: Lay a ball two feet from the hole. Now lay down four more in a straight line at two-foot intervals (illustration 1). Putt the ball nearest the hole, then the second and so on (2, 3). If you miss any putt, start over. Practice until you've holed all five.

If this becomes too easy, you can make it more difficult by placing three balls at each station. The same rule applies: miss any putt and you start at the beginning.

1

2

3

Use a Ball's Brand Name to Perfect Alignment

Purpose: This drill gives you a great visual aid at address that will help you with alignment and the path of your stroke. It also will help you impart a perfect end-over-end roll on the ball, helping the putt hold its line better. Incidentally, this "drill" is legal and can be used in the normal course of play.

Procedure: When you replace your ball after marking, simply align the brand name of the ball so it points down the line of play (see illustration). When you address the putt, you may not believe what your eyes are telling you at first. Try to swing the putterhead back and through on the line the brand name is indicating.

Note also how the ball rolls after it is struck. If the brand name is rolling perfectly with no deviation, fine. If the brand name wobbles, however, you have imparted sidespin on the ball—usually the result of an outside-to-in stroke.

Use a Piece of String to 'See' the Line

Purpose: All good putters have the ability to gauge the speed and break of the putt and then visualize the ball rolling to the hole. This allows the muscles to respond to the image formed in your mind, and results in more consistent putts from all distances.

Procedure: Place your ball on a fairly steep sidehill slope on the putting green. Putt until you hole a ball, noting the path the ball traveled en route to the hole. Study its line and stroke some more putts, aligning your body and the putterface with the starting direction of the ball.

Repeat the procedure on putts from different angles and on different side slopes, each time forming an accurate assessment of how much the ball will break and how hard you must hit the putt to make the ball die at the hole.

Place Putter Against Left Arm to Simplify Stroke

Purpose: A common cause of poor direction and distance control on putts is hinging the left wrist during the stroke. This "breaking down" action causes the putterhead to twist during the stroke, making it difficult to return the putterface to a square position at impact. The following drill will help you keep your left wrist firm throughout the stroke, giving you the sensation that your arms and shoulders rather than your hands and wrists are controlling the putter. When you adapt the principles of the drill to your normal putting stroke, you'll be more consistent.

Procedure: Grasp the putter with your left hand about eight inches down the grip. With your right hand, press the grip end of the putter against the inside of your left arm so it becomes an extension of the left arm itself (illustration 1). Now hit a series of putts (2, 3), noting it is impossible to fan the clubface open and closed with your hands. When you go back to making your normal putting stroke, try to keep your left wrist "frozen" throughout the stroke as in this drill.

1

2

3

Practice Aiming At a Tee For More Confidence

Purpose: There are days when the hole seems small as a thimble, making even routine putts seem impossible to hole. The following exercise will make the hole seem bigger and will result in more confidence on all putts.

Procedure: Stick a tee in the green and place three balls about two feet away. Aim at the tee until you can hit it several times in a row. Move farther from the tee until you are four feet away. Again, try to strike the tee with every putt. Move farther away at two-foot increments until eventually you are aiming at the tee from 10 feet away.

Repeat this procedure several times. When you go out on the course, the hole is sure to look more like a barrel than a thimble!

Putt With Right Hand Only To Improve Feel

Purpose: If your sense of feel has gone south, this drill will help you get it back. Many tour pros use it when preparing to putt on unfamiliar greens. It will help you regain sensitivity in both hands so you can stroke the ball the proper distance and on the correct line. It will improve your stroke by making the putter swing open on the backswing, return to square at impact and then close on the follow-through.

Procedure: Take 20 or 30 balls to the practice green and, using your right hand only, putt them in succession to a hole 20 to 60 feet away. Holding the putter lightly, set it square to the target at address, allow it to swing open on the backswing (1), back to square at impact and then close on the follow-through (2). Don't be too concerned with accurate direction; concentrate more on rolling the ball the correct distance.

203

Shorten Backswing for More Control

Purpose: If your backswing is too long for a given putt, two negative things can happen. You may decelerate on the downstroke, resulting in poor distance control. Your stroke may become too loose, causing the putterface to twist and send the ball off line. The following drill, used by Bruce Lietzke to regulate the length of his backswing, ensures that you swing the putter back only as far as is absolutely necessary. It is especially effective on putts of eight feet or less.

Procedure: Place a ball about three feet from the hole, marking its position to the side by sticking a tee in the ground. Place another tee in the ground about four inches behind your ball (illustration 1). Now hit some putts. If you swing the putter back too far, it will collide with the tee (2). By shortening the length of your backswing, you'll find it necessary to make a more aggressive stroke through the ball. Hit some more putts, this time from about six feet away. This may require that you increase the distance between the tee and the ball by about three more inches. Again, try to avoid hitting the tee on the backswing.

You may have to vary the distance you place the tee behind the ball, depending on the speed of the green. Practice this regularly, and you'll have fewer three-putt greens.

'Cluster' Putting Improves Feel For Distance

Purpose: Here's a great way to develop a feel for distance and improve your touch. It will help you concentrate on hitting the ball solidly and rolling it smoothly, two important keys in making the ball roll the distance you intend.

Procedure: Take six balls out to the putting green. Putt the first ball about 10 feet to a general area on the green, not to a hole. Now try to hit the next five putts the exact same distance as near to the first putt as possible. Gradually increase the distance you hit your first putt, eventually putting the six balls about 50 feet (see illustration).

Putt With Left Hand Only For Better Control

Purpose: Stroking putts with your left hand only will strengthen your left hand and forearm, increasing your control of the putter. It trains you to keep the putter blade moving toward the target, guided by the back of your left hand. When you go back to putting with two hands, your left hand and wrist won't break down and you'll hit your putts more solidly.

Procedure: Using your left hand only, hit a series of two-foot putts, concentrating on accelerating the putter through the ball with the back of your left hand moving directly at the hole. Eventually increase the length of the putts to 10 feet (see illustrations), practicing until you can make a few from the longer distances.

Putt Between Two Clubs to Check Alignment, Stroke

Purpose: There are two areas of putting where golfers most frequently go wrong: Either their putterface isn't square to the target at address, or else their putting swing path is excessively inside-to-out or vice versa. The following drill enables you to check both.

Procedure: Find a straight, level part of the practice putting green. Test this by hitting a few practice putts. Lay two clubs on the green parallel to the line of play and to each other, just far enough apart to accommodate the putterhead (illustration 1). Address a ball, taking special care to see that the putterface is aligned at the target. Now compare the putterface to the clubshafts. It should be perpendicular, or at a right angle, to the clubs. Adjust if it is not.

Now make your normal putting stroke. If the putterhead moves only slightly inside the shaft nearest your feet on the backswing, fine (see illustration 2). Any more than that, and the path is too much to the inside. Note also whether it drifts too far to the outside and adjust accordingly. On the follow-through, the putter should travel directly at the hole (3).

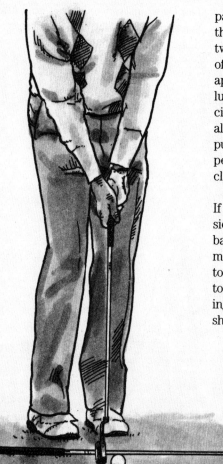

1

Lifting Your Head? Putt With Your Left Eye Closed

Purpose: Lifting your head isn't dangerous in the full swing alone. If you steal a glance at where a putt is rolling before you've completed the stroke, your body as well as your head will move, causing the putter to move off-line. The following drill, popularized by two-time U.S. Open champion Andy North and 1988 Players Championship winner Mark McCumber, will train you to keep your head and body still throughout the stroke. It also will force you to keep your attention focused on the stroke itself, reducing the anxiety which arises from wondering whether the ball will fall into the hole.

Procedure: First make several practice strokes with your left eye closed. Now address a putt, making sure you are aligned correctly and that you have a good mental picture of the hole. Close your left eye. Note that you can't see the hole with your left eye closed. To stroke the putt on the correct line and with proper speed, you'll have to rely on the picture provided by your brain. Go ahead and hit the putt and several more, keeping your right eye glued to the ball until the stroke is completed.

Listen but Don't Look

Purpose: Here's another drill that is effective in preventing you from lifting your head prematurely during the putting stroke. You'll find it is especially difficult on short putts. Gary Player sometimes actually putts in this manner.

Procedure: Hit a series of putts from inside 10 feet, each time keeping your head down until you hear the ball hit the bottom of the cup (See illustrations). To make an appreciable number of putts in this way, your alignment and feel for distance must be accurate.

No

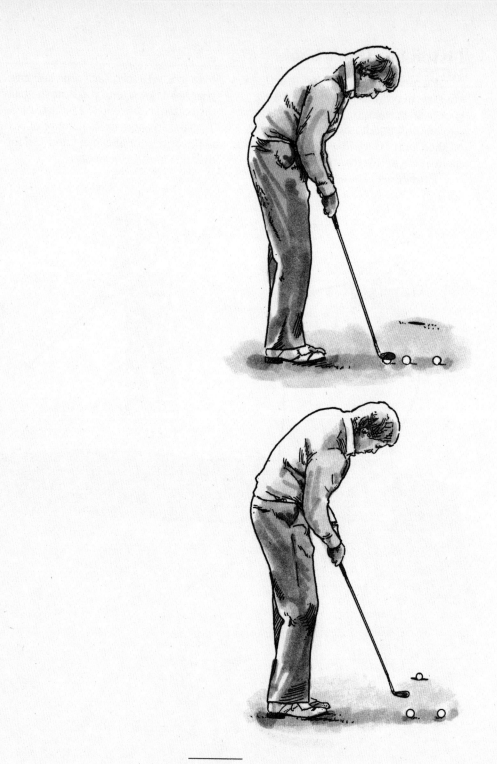

Putt With Your Wedge to Build A Repetitive Stroke

Purpose: Like the last two drills, this one is effective in teaching you to keep your head steady until you've actually struck the ball. This one, however, has two additional benefits. It will develop your hand-eye coordination, which is so important in the delicate area of putting. And it demands great concentration to hit the ball solidly. It also comes in handy for special shots from off the green.

Procedure: Using your sand wedge, address the ball with the leading edge of the clubhead aimed at the ball's equator (illustration 1). This requires that you suspend the clubhead off the ground and support its weight with your arms and hands. Stroke the putt softly to a hole a couple of feet away. You'll find it necessary to keep your head steady and your eyes riveted on the back of the ball. Gradually increase the distance of the putt.

5

DEVELOP YOUR COMPETITIVE INSTINCTS

A very wise man once noted that every golfer has three swings—his practice swing without a ball, his swing on the practice range and his swing on the golf course when every stroke counts. Unfortunately, each one of those swings usually gets progressively worse.

The secret to playing golf well, then, is making your on-course swing as similar as possible to your practice swing. One of the best ways, maybe the only way, to do this is to develop your competitive instincts. This is an area of golf instruction that has, in my opinion, been sorely neglected.

The ability to compete and perform well in pressure situations is relatively as critical to the weekend player as it is to the PGA Tour professional. Everybody wants to win, whether it be the U.S. Open, the club tournament or a Saturday Nassau bet. Consequently, everybody feels some pressure on the golf course and many, if not most of us, choke to a degree and don't perform at our best.

This is primarily a mental thing, of course, a state of mind. But the mind can be trained just as well as the body. In this chapter I have incorporated some drills and a couple of mental exercises that will help you do just that. Breeding competitive instincts in practice will help you develop them in actual play. That will help you perform, whether it be on a full swing or a short putt, as well on the course as you do when there is nothing at stake. It will help you develop the mental toughness you need when it counts.

IMPROVING YOUR COMPETITIVE SKILLS

'100 Percent Drill' Makes Practice Productive

Purpose: Most of your practice time is spent alone. The following drill is a great way to keep you motivated and give yourself a little competition. It will increase your concentration and give you more confidence when you get on the course.

Procedure: Take your shag bag out to the practice green. Choose a hole perhaps 15 feet away. Give yourself a good lie and chip a ball to the hole, trying to hole the shot. If you actually chip it in, score it as minus 1. If you miss, take your putter and try to make the putt. If you make the putt, score it as 0 for getting up and down. If you take two putts, score it as plus 1.

Your goal, of course, is keep your score at 0 or less. If, after chipping and putting 10 balls, you are at plus 1, you have scored "90 percent" and are a first-rate chipper and putter. A score of 0 or better rates as "100 percent," which is of professional quality. That should be your goal. If you are less than 90 percent, this part of your game needs work if you are to be a top player.

Chip 'n Putt To Improve Performance Under Pressure

Purpose: When you are under pressure in a tournament, it is imperative that you maintain your ability to get up and down from around the greens. For many players, the short game is the area that suffers most when the heat is on. The following game provides you with a variety of chips and short putts and will help you execute them better when it counts most. Remember, nothing discourages an opponent more than seeing you get up and down consistently.

Procedure: You'll need a partner, preferably one who is approximately your equal. Go to the practice green and determine who has the honor. The first player drops two balls and chips them to a hole. He then putts out. If he chips one in the hole, it counts as 0. Add the total score of both balls. Now the other player chips and putts his two balls, then adds his score.

I strongly recommend that you play for a small amount of money, anywhere from a nickel to a quarter and up per stroke. This will force you to concentrate on every shot and give you incentive to try your best.

Build Confidence by Making 100 Putts In a Row

Purpose: An effective way to build confidence in your stroke is to simply get used to seeing the ball drop into the hole. By building a pattern of success, you'll have a lot more faith and trust in your stroke when you are under pressure in a tournament or match. If you are a dedicated player, the following drill will help you have a positive attitude over short putts when they count most.

Procedure: First of all, do not wear golf shoes, as you will be standing in the same place for an extended period of time and do not want to wear out the green. Measure one putter-length (about 36 inches) from the hole and mark it with a tee. Now take 10 balls and begin putting, trying to make every one. There is one simple rule: You cannot leave the putting green until you make 100 putts in a row. The putts will seem pretty easy at first, but will become harder as you get into 90's.

The next time you face a short putt under pressure, visualize yourself back on the practice putting green performing this drill. The putt will seem like only one of a hundred you have made, and you'll knock it right in the hole.

Play 18 Holes—On the Practice Range

Purpose: This is a fun exercise you can do alone on the practice range. It will increase your imagination and make your practice more productive by encouraging you to think on every shot. You won't spend too much time hitting one club or fall into the "beating balls" syndrome either, because you are changing clubs on every shot.

Procedure: Imagine yourself on the first tee of your home course. If it's a dog-leg-left par 4, for example, take your driver and try to hit the type of shot that would give you the easiest second shot into the green. After you've hit the drive, assess its accuracy and imagine where it would have left you for your second shot. If the shot would have gone into the trees, imagine the type of recovery shot you'd have to play. Now hit your second shot into the "green" and objectively determine where it would have finished. If it would have gone on the green, give yourself a regulation two putts and move to the next "hole." Play 18 holes in this manner and when you're finished, practice the shots that gave you the most trouble. It is important that you leave the range in a positive frame of mind, so try to make real progress in the areas that give you trouble.

Play 'Stymie' to Develop Touch, Concentration

Purpose: There's nothing like competition to sharpen your concentration and touch under pressure. This following game, called "stymie" for obvious reasons, will make you a more effective putter in tournaments and other important rounds. In addition, it's a great gambling game.

Procedure: You need at least two players. The more who play, however, the more fun the game. After determining the order of play, the No. 1 player lags a putt to the first hole. He leaves his ball in place and the rest of the field putts in order. The scoring system:

1. Holing your first putt counts as 0, not 1. A normal two-putt scores 2, and so on.

2. After everyone has hit his first putt, you assess who is closest to the hole, who is second closest, etc. This determines the order for the next hole, with the player closest to the hole putting first, and so on. Whoever has the honor also chooses which hole to putt to.

3. The player closest to the hole then putts first in an attempt to hole out. After that, the player farthest away plays first.

4. If your ball hits another ball, it is a two-stroke penalty. If it hits two balls, it is a four-stroke penalty.

5. If you putt off the green, it is ruled out-of-bounds and you are penalized two strokes. However, you then play your ball from where it lies.

6. Players are allowed to press their ball down to pop it over another ball. A desperation move. As you can see, going last is a big disadvantage as you must go around or miss all balls putted before you.

'Spoke Drill' Improves Short Putting

Purpose: Jack Burke was one of the game's great putters, especially from short range. This drill helped make him deadly from four feet and in. It will improve your touch, concentration, confidence and green reading skills immensely.

Procedure: Select a hole that is situated on the slope of the practice putting green. Place balls on each side of the hole from two feet away. Try to hole all the balls, noting how the break is different on each putt. After you have made all putts three consecutive times each, move the balls to four feet away and repeat the procedure. If you miss one of the balls, begin again.

If you are super-dedicated, you can increase the challenge by making all the putts four consecutive times, or more.

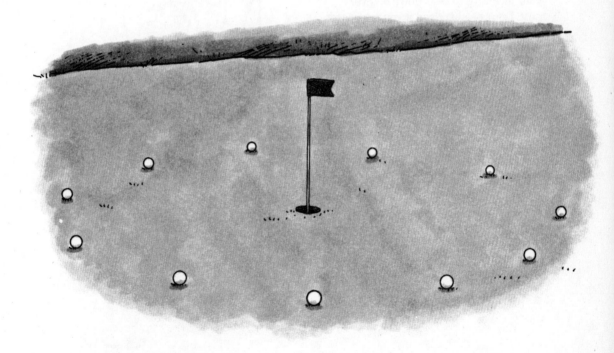

Play 'Lay Back' to Improve Short Putting

Purpose: Here's another game that will improve your putting under pressure, especially in the critical three-to-five-foot range. In addition to making you tougher mentally, it makes practice fun.

Procedure: You need a partner. Putt to any hole and if you fail to sink the putt, move the ball farther back by a full putter length. Your partner putts next and follows the same rule—if he fails to make the putt, he moves it back a putter-length. Low score wins the hole.

I suggest you play for a little something, maybe a quarter a hole. This will increase your incentive to bear down on every putt. Don't be surprised if you take three and four putts on the first few holes!

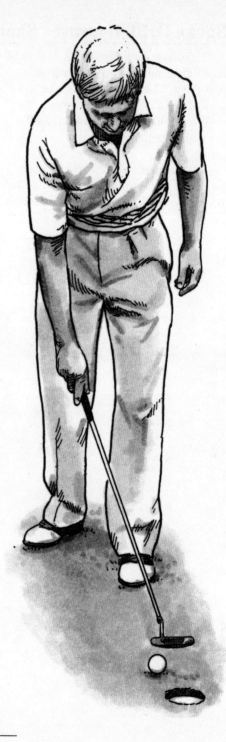

THE MENTAL SIDE OF GOLF

'Test Drill' Improves Your Imagination

Purpose: Every great player has a vivid imagination that enables him to "see" shots coming off before he plays them. Visualizing a swing or a specific ball flight helps you execute a swing much better, especially in delicate situations demanding touch and feel. The following mental exercise will tell you how good your imagination is and will help you improve on it.

Procedure: Close your eyes and imagine you are facing a 20-yard pitch over a bunker to a tightly cut flagstick. Picture yourself playing a fine shot to within a foot of the hole. Now ask yourself these questions:

1. What kind of lie did you have? 2. How high did your shot go? 3. Which way was the wind blowing? 4. Did it affect your shot? 5. How many bounces did the ball take? 6. Did you take a divot?

These are factors to consider on every shot. When you imagined yourself standing over the shot, did you have an accurate picture of each of these considerations? Now picture another shot, this time including all of the factors. Do this drill often, and then use the same process when you face an actual shot on the golf course.

Be Positive

Purpose: This is not so much a drill as a mental practice exercise that has produced great results in many players. It will train you to have a single, positive thought when you stand over the ball, which increases your chances of making a sound, assertive stroke.

Procedure: Toss a ball on the practice green 10 feet from the hole. Assess the line and speed of the putt carefully. Once you have a clear picture of these factors, address the ball with one positive thought, such as a mental picture of the ball falling in the hole. As you stand over the ball, don't allow any negative thoughts, such as, "Have I got the line right?" Rather than *wishing* the ball into the hole, do what you can to *make* it go in the hole.

Don't wait any longer than necessary to stroke the putt. If at any time a negative thought creeps into your mind, step away from the putt and start over. You'll be surprised at how many putts fall while you are thinking assertive, positive thoughts. Simulate a tournament situation so you will get used to thinking positively in competition.